ADVANCE PRAISE FOR

Fight the Power: Breakin Down Hip Hop Activism

"Emerging from intersectional activism inspired and informed by the radical teachings of Hip Hop, this anthology offers first-hand accounts of how Hip Hop culture speaks truth to power taking action to address and eliminate oppression. Extremely timely, *Fight the Power: Breakin Down Hip Hop Activism* is a must read for anyone interested in how diverse scholar-artist activists are taking action in their communities."
— Dr. Johnny Lupinacci, Associate Professor, Washington State University

"Packed with foundational knowledge about hip hop activism that scholars and activists involved in social justice movements must learn, this book is ideal for those seeking a solid introduction to the cultural power of Hip Hop. A timely collection of fascinating interviews that highlights how Hip Hop has inspired a broad range of social change initiatives such as criminal justice reform, youth organizing, and other socio-political issues plaguing communities across the world."
— Dr. Amber E. George, Galen College

"The book is a great step eclectic forward for Transformative Justice! A must read for anyone interested in prison abolition."
— Lucas Alan Dietsche, Former Co-Poet Laureate, Superior, Wisconsin; Editor, Poetry Behind the Walls; Regional Coordinator, Midwest Save the Kids

"This book is timely, provocative, and insightful as it explores and unravels the relations between hip hop and social change. It should be of interest to both hip hop heads and hardcore activists, as well as a general inquisitive public. Definitely worth the read!"
— Dr. Jason Del Gandio, Co-editor, *Spontaneous Combustion: The Eros Effect and Global Revolution*

"This book is a staple for the Hip Hop activist community! Very informative, well written, and educational."
— SouLyricist, CEO, Acoustic Funk Nation; Regional Coordinator, Save the Kids

"This volume centers the political organizing and political values that make hip hop not only a music genre but a movement. The interviews in this volume are essential reading for everyone interested in hip hop, activism, or the complexities of resistance to white supremacy, capitalism, and the state."
— Dr. Sean Parson, Associate Professor of Politics and International Affairs, Northern Arizona University

"Beyond the beat and lyric, *Fight the Power: Breakin Down Hip Hop Activism* boldly shows the kinetic and active forces in Hip Hop that are pushing back on oppressive systems. For the young kids of today, or the aging beatheads, the collection of voices in *Fight the Power: Breakin Down Hip Hop Activism* inspire and educate its audience in creative and empowering ways to utilize their subcultural knowledge to fight back."

—Scott Robertson, Singer, Girlband

"A needed book fighting against the violence of white supremacy."

—*Peace Studies Journal*

"A book of amazing interviews from powerful radical Hip Hop activists that are movers and shakers for social justice and liberation."

—Arissa Media Group

"This book has powerful liberating agency with a genuine Freirean Pedagogy for marginalized groups who use Hip Hop culture to build critical consciousness and activism. It definitely provides a platform and a *voice to the voiceless*, by promoting emancipating pop culture narratives/storytelling that counter narrow-minded views of the world by means of offering social, racial, and economic insights to justice, that forces mainstream society to see the invisible/disenfranchised."

—Dr. Cesar A. Rossatto, Professor, University of Texas, El Paso

"*Fight the Power: Breakin Down Hip Hop Activism* is active resistance, the connecting of souls and communities through shared experiences of invisibility, silencing and hate. *Fight the Power: Breakin Down Hip Hop Activism* allows us to reconnect with our corporal knowledge and those of our ancestors that encountered the same oppression and marginalization for generations. Hip Hop brings us 'home'."

—Chelsie Acosta, National Coordinator, National Week of Action Against
Incarcerating Youth

"Hip Hop paves the way for us to express ourselves in a healthy, positive manner. Through experiences, we are able to tell our story. Through Hip Hop, our voices are heard."

—Voice Of Honey

"This book captures the breath of life, what Native Hawaiians call 'hā' and what indigenous Polynesians call 'manavā,' or power of the breath, through its interview format. Interviews and life writing take us beyond the pure unmitigated 'lines of flight' that Gilles Deleuze couldn't imagine. Its easy-handed editing allows the distillation of the purpose of hip hop: the unmitigated rapture of soul. The end result is direct impact, not only the perpetually-fresh-rooted-to-a-blues-epistemology by a new generation of hip hop artists and activists, but also the impact of highlighting the dispersal of hip hop to the global south, a movement coalescing on the stolen American continent, Turtle Island."

—Dr. Lea Lani Kinikini, Chief Diversity Officer and Special Assistant to the
President for Inclusivity and Equity, Salt Lake Community College

Fight the Power

Hip Hop Studies and Activism

Anthony J. Nocella II, Daniel White Hodge,
Don C. Sawyer III, Ahmad R. Washington,
and Arash Daneshzadeh
Series Editors

Vol. 3

The Hip Hop Studies and Activism series
is part of the Peter Lang Education list.
Every volume is peer reviewed and meets the highest
quality standards for content and production.

PETER LANG
New York • Bern • Berlin
Brussels • Vienna • Oxford • Warsaw

Fight the Power

Breakin Down Hip Hop Activism

Edited by
Arash Daneshzadeh, Anthony J. Nocella II,
Chandra Ward, and Ahmad R. Washington

PETER LANG
New York • Bern • Berlin
Brussels • Vienna • Oxford • Warsaw

Library of Congress Cataloging-in-Publication Control Number: 2021036808

Bibliographic information published by **Die Deutsche Nationalbibliothek.**
Die Deutsche Nationalbibliothek lists this publication in the "Deutsche
Nationalbibliografie"; detailed bibliographic data are available
on the Internet at http://dnb.d-nb.de/.

ISSN 2690-6872 (print)
ISSN 2690-6880 (online)
ISBN 978-1-4331-9108-4 (hardcover)
ISBN 978-1-4331-9013-1 (paperback)
ISBN 978-1-4331-9014-8 (ebook pdf)
ISBN 978-1-4331-9015-5 (epub)
DOI 10.3726/b18583

© 2022 Peter Lang Publishing, Inc., New York
80 Broad Street, 5th floor, New York, NY 10004
www.peterlang.com

This book is dedicated to the late great Albuquerque rapper Wake Self, who was an amazing person, friend to many, and voice against sexism, racism, and police brutality. Wake Self was a perfect example of a Hip Hop activist.

Table of Contents

Foreword

DON C. SAWYER III

I was born on Wednesday, August 11, 1976, in Harlem, NYC and I love to tell my students that I share a birthday with Hip Hop. Many Hip Hop historians mark the birth of Hip Hop on August 11, 1973 when DJ Kool Herc threw his now famous party in the recreation room located at 1520 Sedgwick Avenue. I was born to teen parents a few years before the war on drugs and crack started to destroy my neighborhood. Charting out my life from that point until now, many may have seen me in prison, dead, or living some statistical reality shaped by a deficit perspective and controlling images informed by the dominant narratives of Black masculinity. A Black male, born to teen parents, living in the Abraham Lincoln Housing Projects, on welfare, during the height of the crack cocaine epidemic was not supposed to make it to be a tenured sociology professor. Hip Hop saved my life!

During my third-grade school year, my mother started to notice my behavioral shifts. I started to act out in school and my teachers began to send notes of concern home to my parents. When punishment did not seem to be working, my parents took me to a child psychologist. My mother asked if I needed to speak to someone because I would not share what was going on with her nor my father. They decided to take me to see a mental health professional at Harlem Hospital. I remember drawing pictures, answering questions, and interpreting what I saw in inkblot photos. After meeting with my teachers, parents, and me, the team decided that there was nothing "wrong" with me. They informed my parents that I was experiencing trauma in my neighborhood. Instead of medicating me, they suggested martial arts. My parents signed me up for classes in the Lincoln West Community Center, located on the basement level of our apartment building. I entered as a new member of Harlem GoJu and to my surprise, my Sensei was Master Dave Thomas, also known as Disco Dave, a legendary founding member of Harlem's famous rap group, The Crash Crew. Again, Hip Hop saved my life!

Sensei Dave was the first Hip Hop activist I ever met. I'm not sure the term was used back then, or if he would describe himself in that way, but that is how I see him. After becoming a Black belt, he opened his dojo in Harlem to benefit youth who could not afford the high prices of martial arts instruction in other sections of Manhattan. He charged between \$10–\$15 per month and there were times when some of us could not afford that small fee. However, he never kicked anyone out of class. He knew what was happening in the streets and he knew that keeping us training helped us avoid trouble. His activism was not in the form of marches or releasing political rap songs. He saw a need in his community and used the principles of Hip Hop and martial arts to meet those needs.

My experience with Sensei Dave and his dedication to our Harlem community had a profound impact on my life. I am now a community engaged, Hip Hop generation, sociologist and much of what I do is a result of watching Sensei Dave's selfless service and dedication to uplifting the community. I've been fortunate to use sociology and Hip Hop to bring about research-driven social change while working with marginalized youth in urban schools, men in prison, men and women reentering society after serving time in prison, and Dominican and Haitian youth living in poor sections of the Dominican Republic. I use Hip Hop culture to center the experiences of the most marginalized members of our community. I see Hip Hop is as a tool to speak truth and amplify the voices of those who have been victims of attempts to silence.

The work I've done throughout my life is similar to the engagement of the activist authors in this book. They use Hip Hop activism to transform lives and social institutions. They see Hip Hop as a tool to deconstruct and reconstruct systems of power and oppression and use the culture to strive for liberation. This book is timely. This book is necessary. Youth culture has always been at the forefront of social change. The work discussed in this text is a shining example of the transformative possibilities of Hip Hop activism.

The masterful selection of these personal stories highlights the many ways Hip Hop and activism blend to bring about social change. The authors' examples of infusing Hip Hop into art activism, mindful film production, critical pedagogy, feminist methodology, and political strategy serve as roadmaps for those of us looking to be socially active while staying true to Hip Hop culture. I hope this text serves as a catalyst for self-reflection, personal development, and a dedication to using Hip Hop activism while blazing a path towards justice.

Preface

NATHANIEL "N8" SANDERS AND CLIFTON G. SANDERS

This first-ever monograph about Hip Hop activism is an extraordinary and timely achievement. After more than 40 years, Hip Hop culture is celebrated worldwide by a broad palette of audiences for a variety of reasons. Because of and despite this platform, the activists in this book rightly assert that Hip Hop culture generates and sustains the continual creation, authentic expression and *voice* of marginalized peoples and oppressed communities. At the heart of Hip Hop's phenomenal and enduring legacy are compelling and fearless narratives, innovative beats, passionate dance and musical fusion that communicate the struggles, aspirations and celebrations of real people expressing their true selves, their painful struggles and their hope in the midst of daunting economic and political oppression, police brutality and social disenfranchisement. As several activists in this monograph affirm, Hip Hop culture, originating in Black and Brown communities, enables them to be seen and heard, to be valued according to local criteria, and to proudly assert creativity, genius, art and innovation as worthy of the world's notice. Moreover, this way of being cultivates solidarity with histories and with current activism worldwide for social justice and liberation of all people.

Obviously, all movements must wrestle with the dissonances between stated ideals and the messy realities of their evolution and propagation. Hip Hop activism is no exception. Activism and critique with regard to Hip Hop culture's inner workings continually confront misogyny, violence, commercialism, social responsibility, drug abuse, community values, history and scope, etc. The activists in this monograph provide valuable perspectives on these and other 'internal' tensions and conversations while nevertheless, treasuring Hip Hop culture as a key, if not indispensable, feature of their agenda for social justice and worldwide liberation via movements such as #BlackLivesMatter, antiracism initiatives, education and community development, and transnational collaborations.

As son and father collaborators for this Preface, we would like to offer a personal testimony which attests to the importance of this monograph. In 2015 the son (Nathaniel a freshman college film student at the time), invited the father (Clifton, a scientist/educator who also is a local jazz musician and veteran of funk, soul and gospel bands) to listen to Kendrick Lamar's *To Pimp a Butterfly* CD. This seminal incident profoundly transformed our relationship. Although we are separated in age by 42 years, this encounter began a rich, ongoing dialogue about Hip Hop lyrics, historical and thematic continuity between Hip Hop and other Black music genres, the history and legacy of spoken word-empowered activism across generations (e.g., The Last Poets, Gil Scott-Heron), and how 70's soul music became source material for early NWA productions as portrayed in *Straight Outta Compton* . On car rides, on long road trips, at the movies and on other occasions over the years, Nathaniel shared with Clifton the work of socially conscious Hip Hop artists such as Kendrick Lamar, Joey BadA$$, J Cole, JID, Saba, Noname, Chance the Rapper, Rapsody, and others.

We always discuss at length the lyrics, stories, artistry and social commentary expressed in these recordings. A beautiful thing about our bonding through Hip Hop is how it connects the father's young adulthood listening to artists such as Kurtis Blow, Run DMC, DJ Jazzy Jeff and The Fresh Prince, Queen Latifa, Salt-N-Pepa, and Public Enemy (particularly in the Spike Lee movie *Do The Right Thing*). The father deeply appreciates Hip Hop's willingness to honor and infuse jazz, gospel and soul music in fresh and compelling ways that extend the vital practices and traditions of Black music as social commentary. This gracious dialogue originating in the son's love for Hip Hop has mentored and revived the father. Moreover, these interactions illuminate Nathaniel's evolving politics and activism, including his desire to make films that have deep impact for advancing social justice. As a community college chief academic officer, Hip Hop activism urges Clifton to be more attentive to his responsibilities as he seeks to meet the educational needs of an increasingly culturally and economically diverse Utah college student population. To say the least, it is not a stretch at all to acknowledge the persistent influence of Hip Hop upon our shared outlook and commitments as Black men living in the United States.

Our humble son-father testimonial supports in some way, we hope, the reflections of the activists featured in this monograph. Several share their formative experiences, convictions and their leadership vision in dialogue with their assessment of Hip Hop history and culture. Many freely admit Hip Hop as their passion and inspiration; others seem more circumspect.

Nevertheless, the strength of this monograph is in how the interviews are structured, giving each activist ample opportunity to articulate substantively how Hip Hop informs their praxis. Perhaps most importantly, each interview depicts an extraordinary dedication that flows naturally from the overwhelming love, empathy and compassion that motivates the activists' solidarity and their sacrifices on behalf of the lives, culture and dignity of their beleaguered yet defiant communities. Their work is compelling on several levels, urging us to heed their admonitions about nurturing, listening to and learning from young, dedicated voices. We also need to cherish their conviction that solutions which come from those who are most directly impacted by problematic circumstances and challenges are the wisest solutions.

Today, Hip Hop boasts artists, entertainers, producers and moguls who have global fanbases, enormous and diversified business empires and, as of 2019, a Pulitzer Prize winner in Kendrick Lamar. Elite universities offer courses and support research and scholarship in Hip Hop culture. The global commercial and literary triumph of Hip Hop culture at this moment affords an historic opportunity to hear and (re)connect with the grass roots activists in this monograph, to engage their synthesis of Hip Hop consciousness, narrative, education, community building, social justice and liberation. With joy and hope for healing and change, we commend to you this groundbreaking collection of interviews. Prophesy ...' We gon' be alright'!!

Acknowledgements

We would like to thank all the individuals in the book that were interviewed and wrote for the book and who are beautiful examples of Hip Hop activists—Don C. Sawyer III, Clifton G. Sanders, Nathaniel "N8" Sanders, Lauren Leigh Kelly, Eli Jacobs-Fanatuazzi, "Mic" Crenshaw, Reies Romero, Katrina Benally, Selinda Guerrero, Antonio Quintana, Jared A. Ball, and David Michael. We would like to thank everyone that gave praise for the book as well—Dr. Johnny Lupinacci, Dr. Amber E. George, Lucas Alan Dietsche, Dr. Jason Del Gandio SouLyricist, Dr. Sean Parson, Scott Robertson, Peace Studies Journal, Arissa Media Group, Dr. Cesar A. Rossatto, Chelsie Acosta, and VoiceOfHoney. We would like to thank the many organizations that supported the creation of this book including Save the Kids, Peace Studies Journal, Academy for Peace Education, Institute for Critical Animal Studies, Journal of Hip Hop Studies, Hip Hop Studies and Activism Book Series, Poetry Behind the Walls, Arissa Media Group, Green Theory and Praxis Journal, Critical Animal Studies Association, Critical Animal Studies Society, Utah Reintegration Program, Utah Criminology Student Association, Student Organization for Animal Rights, Houston Animal Rights Team, Vegan Outreach, Salt Lake Youth Open Mic, and Utah Prisoner Letter Writing. Arash would like to thank his students at USF UC Davis and San Francisco Unified School District for their willingness to explore hip hop as a vehicle for change. Additionally Arash will like to thank and acknowledge all the fallen victims to police brutality and activist MCs for inspiring this educational abolitionist work. Chandra thanks her wife Eli, Family and friends. Ahmad would like to thank the Creator, Ancestors, his family, friends and Hip Hop. Finally, we would like to thank everyone in Hip Hop that protects it, makes it grow, and loves it.

Introduction

The Emergence of the 11th Element
of Hip Hop

ARASH DANESHZADEH, ANTHONY J. NOCELLA II, CHANDRA
WARD, AND AHMAD WASHINGTON

DEFINING HIP HOP ACTIVISM

Hip Hop was founded in the 1970s in the Bronx, New York with only four elements—breakdancing, DJing, graffiti, and MCing. Then emerged Beatboxing, Hip Hop *fashion*, Hip Hop Language, Hip Hop *Knowledge*, Hip Hop *Entrepreneurialism*, and health and wellbeing. Most recently, people have been claiming themselves as Hip Hop activists has always been around, but Save the Kids, Youth Justice Coalition, Black August, Rock the Vote, and Malcolm X Grassroots Movement. Hip Hop activism is introducing Hip Hop elements into classic tactics and strategies for social justice. For example rather than just speakers at a protest they would have spoken-word artist or an MC performing. Further, rather than professional corporate banners designed for the protest, graffiti artists would design and make the banners, posters, logos, signs, shirts, and maybe even chalk on the sidewalk and street and at the protest there would be Hip Hop music.

On the opposite side, Hip Hop activism is also about introducing socio-political and economic issues to Hip Hop communities such as having a table with political literature at a music show or breakdance contest. Moreover, rap lyrics that are political, wearing political shirts at a concert, graffiti on walls with political messages, protesting a Hip Hop artist such as Iggy Azalea by Save the Kids in Minneapolis, Minnesota, which aided her in canceling her show at that location, and speaking on political issues between music artists at a concert about such issues as police brutality, poverty, suicide, sexual assault, and veganism. Hip Hop activists are the individuals that keep those in the culture in check, by publicly questioning artists and leaders such as R. Kelly with his sexual assault accusations and Kayne West with his praise for over a year of Donald Trump.

Therefore, Hip Hop activism is about Hip Hop introduced to politics or politics introduced to Hip Hop. The culture of Hip Hop activism is creative, free flowing, raw, in your face, not humble, blatant, confident, honest, passionate, emotional, circular, not professional, not detached, not objective, but subjective, engaged, participatory, networking, coalition building, community building, and holistic in that it is about the mind, body, and spirit.

PURPOSE OF THE BOOK

The goal and hopes of this book is to educate people on how Hip Hop is a culture, strategy, and tactic for social change. Hip Hop can be funny, political, social, sexual, racial, youthful, classy, and classist. The question is how do activism from Standing Rock and Black Lives Matter, to name just two movements, utilize Hip Hop in their chants, banners, flyers, website, organizing, and addressing conflict? Hip Hop can be political and some even argue is always political, while some say Hip Hop does not necessarily need or have to be political, but rather can be offensive or simply fun to party to. For example Will Smith aka the Fresh Prince did not need to change his style at all to be financially successful and publicly popular, as he was a Hip Hop artist that was always about fun and not politics. On the other hand Ice Cube from the group NWA had to do change completely from being a hardcore gangsta raw rapper to a clean-cut Sunday afternoon family friend G-rated comedian that you could watch on the Disney Channel. For almost a dedicate his raw politic attitude was invisible to the public, until he became noted as one of the top actors and one could refer to him as making it. It was after he made it that he became political again. One could say that was strategic and another is being opportunist as him becoming political was at the same time Black Lives Matter erupted.

Hip Hop activism is just that activism with the presence of Hip Hop. Activism is the strategic escalation of a conflict to raise awareness in-order to create social change. Some examples of activism is boycotts, protests, sit-ins, hunger-strikes, fasts, die-ins, blockades, civil disobedience, tree sits, banner drops, marches, press conferences, vigils, noise demonstrations, occupations, chalk-ins, critical masses, twitter bombs, call-ins, petitions, letter writing, rallies, and social change can throughout history occurred through violence as well such as armed struggle, revolution, riots, rebellions, battles, and war. Hip Hop activism is the inserting of Hip Hop by those that are authentically Hip Hop into activism tactics noted above.

OUTLINE OF BOOK

In the first chapter, university professor and founder of the Hip Hop Youth Summit Lauren Leigh Kelly recalls her entrée into the Hip Hop community through the element of DJ'ing eventually leading her to become a Hip Hop educator. Kelly discusses the role of Hip Hop in her activist organizing and teaching praxis. Reflecting on Hip Hop activists that have inspired her, highlights some of the tensions facing Hip Hop today and its implications in the evolution of Hip Hop as a culture.

Documentary filmmaker, Eli Jacobs-Fantauzzi discusses the role activism and Hip Hop has played in his personal life and art in Chapter Two. We get to follow his evolution as a filmmaker, scholar and activist from the ivory towers of America to the streets of Columbia. Here Jacobs-Fantauzzi gives us a closer look into his projects that have taken him around the world and where a trip to Ghana forever changed his life.

In Chapter Three, we get to take a peek into rapper, poet, and social justice educator "Mic" Crenshaw's journey into Hip Hop and activism. From his formative years in Minneapolis as a founder of a SHARP (skinheads against racial prejudice) collective taking down local Nazis to building alliances with local Hip Hop crews, we follow Crenshaw's journey into anti-racism organizing and his love for Hip Hop. Currently based out of Portland, Oregon the artist continues to build with Hip Hop artists from around the globe and inspire and develop youth in his community Crenshaw's story is certainly a unique one.

In Chapter Four, Minnesota based DJ Reiss Romero discusses the importance of the element of DJ'ing to Hip Hop culture and its influence on his how personal growth and development. Reflecting back on his journey to becoming a DJ, Romero reveals how Hip Hop is inherently educational and that this be can used as a vehicle by which to connect with youth, just as it did when he was younger. As an educational tool, Hip Hop has the power to challenge white supremacy and connect with kids who have been failed by the mainstream educational system.

In Chapter Five, musician Katrina Benally shares with us memories of their evolving love for music. Intersections of gender, sexuality and race are explored in how these identities have presented challenges breaking into the rap game as well as how they inform and shape their music. Occupying multiple marginalized identities, even within Hip Hop, activism comes in many forms such as rejecting misogyny and demanding respect from her male peers in the Hip Hop scene.

Activist Selinda Guerrero recounts how activism has always been a part of her life, in Chapter Six. From a very young age, Guerrero interacted with the criminal justice system. This interaction had an indelible effect on her helping to inform her activism and activist identity. She discovered Hip Hop can speak to her oppression as a woman of color on all dimensions and sees Hip Hop as a place of refuge for herself and other folks with marginalized identities.

In Chapter Seven, Tony Quintana opens up about the deep influence Hip Hop had on him growing up. Hip Hop as a place of refuge, a place from which to draw strength is something Quintana identified early on in the music and the culture. This emcee sees the almost inherent ability of Hip Hop to amplify marginalized voices and uses his talent as an emcee and Hip Hop as the vehicle to do this as a source of empowerment.

In the last chapter, Jared A. Ball discusses the role Hip Hop has played in his life as well as its current role in politics. With the ruling political parties threatening to co-opt Hip Hop to advance their own purposes, he reflects on the true meaning of Hip Hop activism. Ball begs us to interrogate how Hip Hop activism can truly be activist within a system of capitalism and mainstream liberal politics dictating current Hip Hop culture.

We hope the reader is motivated for action from this book and finds an organization or builds an organization grounded in Hip Hop activism. This book is the first book in the world about Hip Hop activism and we hope this will not be the last. We do not believe this is the bible of Hip Hop activism or that we believe we have addressed every concern and topic related to Hip Hop activism. We believe that interviewing those that are Hip Hop activists are the best way in introducing a new concept to the world. We do argue that are Hip Hop activists, but we also know we are academics and as such we have a responsibility such as Howard Zinn mentored academics to do, is provide space and place for the marginalized and those in the trenches of social change. We hope this book sparks a fire for true global revolutionary change and transformative justice.

CHAPTER ONE

Interview with Lauren Leigh Kelly

ANTHONY J. NOCELLA II

Anthony: Can you tell me, in detail, your story about how you got involved in the Hip Hop community, and if you can, share with us some of your first memorable moments when you joined the Hip Hop community on an active level?

Lauren: What an interesting question. I feel as though I've always been involved in the Hip Hop community in some way. However, that also depends on how we are defining Hip Hop community, which is large and broad. I grew up listening to Hot 97 (a New York City-Hip Hop/R&B radio station) and at that time it felt like a community that I was a part of. I especially remember the show "Street Soldiers" hosted by Lisa Evers on Sunday nights at 9pm. It was an hour-long discussion of issues and perspectives impacting the Black community. Listening to that program taught me early on that 'it was much bigger than Hip Hop' (shout out to Dead Prez) and that I was a part of an engaged community. It also taught me a lot about the role of dialogue in developing understandings about social issues and community issues.

I remember Lisa Evers would provide the topic and callers would offer their perspectives and ideas. They didn't necessarily come to a clear solution each time, but I felt like the conversation always moved us further in the direction of solutions, which is what dialogue does. When I think about it, listening to that program from such an early age may have helped me to develop many of my approaches to teaching, which are also dialogic and inquiry-based.

As an undergrad, I started DJ-ing at college parties and events. In that way I felt like I was able to take an active role in selecting the music I listened to and, thereby, the ideologies I aligned myself with. At that time, there was a lot of misogynistic and homophobic mainstream Hip Hop music on the radio, and it felt powerful to be able to resist that by playing music that felt uplifting to me. It was also cool to be part of a DJ community. It meant that wherever I went- across cities, states, and countries, I had immediate family in other DJ's, record store owners, and Hip Hop heads- we were linked and we held each other down (or up?). I recall this happening in Connecticut when I first began dji-ng and also in England and Japan when I moved there. Through dj-ing, I found community really quickly in those places, and in ways that allowed me to develop really meaningful connections with people and places. I also had a Hip Hop show around that time at an AM radio station that was rooted both in the college and the local community. It was a strange experience because I was alone in a room with a microphone assuming people were listening but never really knowing. During one show, I read a passage that I found powerful from a book that I was reading by H. Rap Brown. After I read it over the air, I immediately started receiving phone calls from listeners who were moved by the passage. That was a really pivotal moment for me because I realized that even though I was alone in a room with records and a mic, I wasn't alone at all. There were people listening on the other end and what I played and said reached them.

As an educator, I became deeply involved in the Hip Hop education and spoken word communities, which intersect a great deal, especially in New York City. Through these communities, I have become connected to a group of genuine, committed youth and colleagues who are actively working towards equity and social justice through the arts, through music, through community activism, and who share my passion for hip hop and love for Black people and people of color. I know when I go to events organized by people within these communities that I am learning from and with them and from trailblazers who have been doing this work and who are cultivating youth leadership in creative and transformative ways. I also know when I walk into these spaces that I am seeing my family- whether or not we've ever met before.

Anthony: What does Hip Hop mean to you, and can you provide a few examples of how Hip Hop has challenged, changed, and influenced society as a whole globally?

Lauren: I think Hip Hop is about connecting to the self and to others. Since I was introduced to Hip Hop by my brother, it was a part of our connection to each other. Many of my students often cite parents, cousins, friends, and siblings as their introduction to Hip Hop as well. It's a type of gift that loved ones can pass on to each other. I think because Hip Hop is so deeply rooted in self-expression and authenticity, there is a vulnerability in sharing your connection to Hip Hop with others and so that willingness to share that with someone shows your trust in them and your love for them. Sometimes, knowing the ways in which another person engages with Hip Hop can tell you much more about them than they perhaps could describe in words; it's a way of showing your consciousness since Hip Hop is way of knowing and being. For example, if I start a line from a Hip Hop song and you finish it, then we're already connected. We know each other. I would argue that that is especially true for those of previous Hip Hop genera-tions. Currently, Hip Hop culture has become so mainstream and synonymous with popular culture that finishing a Biggie line doesn't necessarily mean what it used to. I think we are at a point where a person can actively listen to rap music and at the same time not connect to it, and as a Hip Hop head I'm still trying to make sense of that.

We see this shift especially with Hip Hop music. Previously, there were so many more barriers to becoming famous in Hip Hop that doing so meant you had a great deal of talent and support. You also tended to have more longevity as an artist. Currently, there are so many sources and mechanisms for creating and distributing music that there is wonderfully more to choose from, but Hip Hop fame tends to be much more short-lived. The same goes for language, fashion, and other trends within Hip Hop. Everything is moving so quickly that it's harder to really pin down what and who is and isn't Hip Hop. There is something both fascinating and unsettling about that.

Putting that tension aside, however, I think that the power of Hip Hop as a culture and community is about connecting with the lives and stories of people who you may have never met, but who you feel you know and who understand you. And I think that is consistent throughout each of the elements of Hip Hop. Graffiti, for example, is very much about community- building upon one anoth-er's ideas and creativity, competing with each other, learning and developing as an artist by observing the work of other artists. And I think that's consistent in DJ-ing, emceeing, and b-boying. Something I've been sitting with recently is the role of the 5th element of Hip Hop in culture and community. In many ways, knowledge of self is amorphous because it is subjective and introspective. At the same time, I wonder if there are ways to think more explicitly about what knowledge of self looks like on a wider scale. For example, what does it mean for a community of people to know themselves as a community? And then how can we both preserve and build upon that knowledge? In some ways, archiving Hip Hop music and culture is a form of that, but I don't think there's a clear connection to the consciousness part of that yet.

I think that one challenge that Hip Hop has presented to the world is that it forced mainstream society to see us. And by "us" I mean oppressed people, Black and brown people, marginalized people- beautiful, intelligent, resourceful people who refuse to be ignored. It has also provided a "voice for the voiceless" and a vehicle for mobilization and social change. I think we've seen this in urban areas of the U.S. but we've also seen it in Brazil, Cuba, Palestine, France, etc. Hip Hop has really grown to represent not only resistance to the status quo but also a shift in the status quo.

In terms of change and influence, that's something I'm still trying to work through. I love that Hip Hop has become so popular and influential- it's in the White House; it's in academia; it's on Broadway. And I think that is so powerful and wonderful. At the same time, it raises some complex tensions. When Hip Hop enters new spaces, especially spaces that have historically excluded the same identities that gave rise to Hip Hop, something is going to change. Hip Hop can't exist in the same way that it has once it's in these spaces, and I think we're in a moment when we're still not sure how to navigate that. I think about Kendrick Lamar's album cover for "To Pimp a Butterfly" portraying him and other Black men and children in front of the White House. It is a revolutionary notion; but at the same time, Hip Hop has been in the White House so much in the past decade that it's not quite as jaw-dropping an idea as it once was. This means something. I think what we need to keep asking ourselves, however, is how that meaning is shifting over time. While the goal may at one point have been Hip Hop getting the invite to the White House, now that the invites are coming, what does Hip Hop do while it's there? I think that's the question we really need to be asking as Hip Hop increasingly becomes absorbed into mainstream, popular culture.

Anthony: While many believe Hip Hop is political, very few identify themselves as a Hip Hop activist. Can you explain what Hip Hop activism is and is not and give examples of it? Who are key individuals that should be noted as key founders and mentors of Hip Hop activism and why?

Lauren: I think that Hip Hop activism can take many forms. It can be creating music that fosters critical consciousness, listening to and sharing music that fosters that consciousness, or supporting it in other ways. It could be tapping into the Hip Hop community to organize and build movements. It could be expressing your Hip Hop identities while engaging in activism. I'm not sure we can define it. I think that Hip Hop activism is not creating, supporting, or promoting music, structures, people, or ideas that participate in oppression, marginalization, dehumanization, disenfranchisement, or assault.

When I think of Hip Hop activism I think of KRS One, MC Lyte, Queen Latifah, Sister Soulja, Talib Kweli, Mos Def, Kendrick Lamar, Public Enemy, Common, Dead Prez, Nas. I also think of Colin Kaepernick, Tricia Rose, Martha Diaz, Michael Eric Dyson, bell hooks. In more recent examples, I think of

J. Cole as an artist, co-conspirator, and public figure; Jay-Z co-producing the Kalief Browder documentary and supporting 21 Savage's legal defense as he dealt with ICE in 2019; A Tribe Called Quest's last album; Joey Bada$$'s last album, and Janelle Monae's participation in #BlackLivesMatter protests. The list is expansive and I don't know if we can pinpoint a select group of individuals because Hip Hop is nothing without its community of participants. I also don't think Hip Hop activism exists without the work of Black feminist movements (i.e. #Blacklivesmatter), the Black Panther Party, civil rights activists, and the Black Liberation struggles that have occurred both domestically and globally.

I think that the line between being political and being an activist is vague. If an artist is sharing ideas through a hip hop-based medium, I see that as activism, even if they are not organizing a panel or protest or even participating in a panel or protest. There are so many ways to engage with ideas and to work towards equity and I think labels matter much less than your words and actions.

Anthony: What issues, tactics, and strategies make Hip Hop activism different than other forms of activism such as feminism, LGBTTQQIA, disability activism, animal rights activism, environmentalism, social justice activism, anti-war activism, vegan activism, food justice, environmental justice, transgender activism, transnational feminism, and decolonizing activism?

Lauren: I'm not sure if it is different. I see Hip Hop activism *as* social justice activism. I think it includes feminism and decolonizing activism. What makes Hip Hop distinct is perhaps the language that's used and the ability to reach diverse generations and communities through music, celebrity, and popular culture. And what's interesting about that is the language and look can be off-putting to some while drawing in others. So when Hip Hop is saying "F- the police," we're saying that we need to dismantle a racist system that unjustly and disproportionately polices Black and Brown bodies. If you don't understand the language of Hip Hop, you don't hear that. You might instead hear a threat against individual police officers or disorganized anger. But it's resistance and Hip Hop becomes the organization. When Dead Prez criticizes the education system in "They Schools," they're talking about school reform. We see much less of this now, but in the first 2 decades of Hip Hop we saw women such as Lady Pink, Queen Latifah, Roxanne Shante, and Monie Love advocating for feminism. Again, the medium through which these messages come is non-traditional. It may not be a t-shirt or a poster, but that doesn't make it any less political or active.

Another thing to consider is that Hip Hop also helps to provide the context for these movements. The imagery and narratives of Hip Hop illustrate these issues. Through Hip Hop music and culture, we see the effects of war, of food deserts, of low-income families being forced to live near factories and in the most polluted areas of our cities. Hip Hop helps to galvanize individuals and communities around particular issues and it can foster empathy. I remember when the *Hip Hop for Respect* album came out in 2000. I was aware of the shooting of Amadou Diallo and that this was certainly not new, but hearing that project, which was dedicated to resisting police violence and raising awareness, also taught me about particular tools of activism in the Hip Hop community. Sometimes, it's artists collaborating on an album and telling their stories. The song "Self-Destruction," of course, is another example of this, with artists such as KRS-ONE, MC Lyte, Heavy D, and Public Enemy collaborating on an activist-oriented track.

Anthony: How long have you been doing Hip Hop activism and in what ways have you engaged in Hip-Hop activism? Can you tell us some successful Hip Hop activist events you have organized and participated in and why they were successful in your opinion?

Lauren: I don't separate my Hip Hop identity from my activism, so I would say I've been engaged in Hip Hop activism for as long as I've been engaged with Hip Hop - since childhood. As I mentioned, listening to the radio, becoming a DJ, hosting a radio show, were all forms of activism for me. Since becoming an educator, my activism has primarily been through my teaching, writing, work with youth and pre-service teachers, and community building. I do a lot of work with critical Hip Hop literacies in the classroom. This means bringing Hip Hop texts such as songs, articles, videos, and films into the classroom for the purpose of engaging in critical dialogue about the texts. Specifically, I engage my students in explicit conversations around race, class, gender, power, and sexuality through the lens of these texts. What I love about this work is that I am learning all the time. Louise Rosenblatt wrote about what she terms "transactional theory," or the idea that meaning occurs in the transaction between the reader and the text, rather than existing in the text itself. What that means in the classroom is that the conversations are new every time. Each person has their own reading of the text and we put these perspectives in conversation with one another so that we are all developing understandings throughout the discussion. And of course our perspectives are impacted by our own identities so the conversations inevitably delve into individual identities and experiences. Because Hip Hop music and culture contain implicit and explicit symbols of power, race, class, gender, and sexuality, classroom discussion of Hip Hop becomes a discussion of these symbols and the ideologies that Hip Hop reflects, resists, and shapes. That's where this critical consciousness work happens - through those conversations and the development of complex understandings of our social world.

An event that I organize annually is the Hip Hop Youth Summit. It's a workshop that I began when I started teaching Hip Hop literature to high school students. The idea is to bring together students of Hip Hop, Spoken Word, and/or social justice to engage with the elements of Hip Hop, to develop skills in critical literacy, and to build coalitions with one another. Each year, students come from a diversity of schools, both urban and suburban, to learn from Hip Hop scholars and activists, learn more about Hip Hop and activism, and to explore their individual roles as leaders and change-makers. Past speakers and workshop leaders include Dr. Christopher Emdin, Professor of science education; Dr. Ernest Morrell, Professor of English education; Dr. Nicole Mirra, Professor of Urban Education; Toni Blackman, Poet, Rapper, actor and Hip Hop Ambassador; Michael Cirelli, Executive Director of Urban Word NYC; Martha Diaz founder of the H2Ed Center at NYU; Andrew Carter, choreographer; Kristy Leibowitz, photographer; Mikal Amin Lee, emcee, writer, educator, and curator; Sam Sellers, emcee, DJ, and educator; Sofia Snow, Deputy Director of Urban Word NYC; and Justis Lopez, educator, DJ, and consultant. What's great about having this diversity of speakers is that it provides the students with a range of examples of ways to be involved in activism and in Hip Hop. It also shows them that there are unique ways to blend your creativity and your passions with your professional life. What I love about this event is seeing the students from different schools connect to and learn from one another. I don't think young people get enough opportunities to do that.

I am currently in the process of building this work out into an annual Hip Hop Youth Research and Activism Conference. The idea behind this is that young people are more appropriately positioned to be the leaders and thinkers in their own lives and communities than those of us who are further away from the immediate realities of being young. Paulo Freire talked about this when he wrote about the revolution needing to include the "oppressed" as thinkers and not solely as "doers." If it is only the adult allies, or grown-ups who take on leadership positions in social justice movements, then we are not really doing the work. We must be working alongside our youth rather than for or on behalf of them. I think that Hip Hop as a community and culture offers a really powerful space for youth activism and the conference becomes the catalyst for solidarity to be built amongst young people from diverse backgrounds and communities. This is also an intergenerational space that includes middle school, high school, and college students. So again, it doesn't position the youngest as doers being led by those who are more experienced. Rather, we are looking to build a community of folks at different places in their academic and social education who can learn from and with each other. This involves having young people volunteer to collaborate on building the conference- conceiving and executing the vision and design; reviewing proposals for the conference, mentoring workshop leaders in building powerful, engaged sessions. This is work that is layered, complex, difficult, and absolutely beautiful. As this conference grows, the notion is that the art, activism, and research foci of the conference begin to intersect really organically. Scholar, writer, and educator Dr. Bettina Love once said that the revolution cannot exist without art, and the purpose of this conference is to organize our youth to build community and action out of that idea.

Anthony: In what ways do you see Hip Hop activism growing and being needed in society and within the realm of Hip Hop? What are some campaigns that Hip Hop activists are pushing and working on right now and should be working on now or in the future?

Lauren: Because Hip Hop has grown to be so popular and mainstream, especially among younger folks, I think we have a really ripe opportunity to draw young people into the community as activists. I had a conversation with the students in my Hip Hop literature class once in which many of them said that socially conscious music isn't for the "radio" (inclusive of popular streaming devices) or for mainstream audiences. I had to remind them that in the 90s, socially conscious music was mainstream and on the radio. It was the music that I grew up on. To some degree, I must attribute much of my activist spirit to growing up through Nas, Common, Queen Latifah, Mos Def, and others. The idea that music can be uplifting, empowering, critically conscious, and commercially successful is not foreign to me and I think that we are seeing that happen again with artists such as J. Cole. The fact that he collaborates a lot of with younger artists is also a really powerful example of how important it is to involve young people in Hip Hop activism and that this must happen by building intergenerational communities, rather than isolating those who don't share our views or experiences.

I also think it's important to take note that of this moment in which so many people from outside of the Hip Hop community are wanting to join it and profit off of it. I think we need to challenge them to see us again (see question 2 for details), to see our stories and our struggles, to acknowledge their complicity in these struggles, and to do something about it. During a panel discussion on the use of the "N" word in Hip Hop, rapper Immortal Technique once said, "You can't love our music without loving our people." That really resonated with me. I think we have a lot of people loving the music without understanding it, and without loving those who create it. I would love to see mainstream Hip Hop embrace the #Blacklivesmatter movement and the struggle for social justice. Through that, I think we can build a larger community of activists who are fighting with love and resisting the colonization of Hip Hop and of our communities.

I see this work happening to some degree with popular artists such as Kendrick Lamar and Chance the Rapper, who find ways to maintain commercial success while subverting the traditional avenues for commercial success. While Chance's music itself doesn't engage explicitly with these issues, his actions as a public figure have drawn attention to the need to focus on education and rebuilding communities. Kendrick analyzes complex issues of race, class, power, and identity in his music and I think it provides a great example for others who want to do similar work. I think social media has also been instrumental in developing a Hip Hop activist citizenry. Aside from #BLM, I'd really love to see more attention paid to Black feminism and intersectionality. I think that can only happen if we have more mainstream female artists and an audience that will support that.

CHAPTER TWO

Interview with Eli Jacobs-Fantauzzi

ARASH DANESHZADEH

Arash: What inspired or catalyzed your place behind the camera?

Eli: I remember the more I started filming things the more I fell in love with it. My mother bought her first camcorder when I was in high school. After using it the first few times I could not put the camera down. I couldn't leave the house without it. I started documenting everything around me, which included Hip Hop shows, student protests, and the organizing behind the scenes.

When I went to college, I didn't really know what I wanted to study. It wasn't until my senior year that I took my first official film class with Dr. Loni Ding, a professor in the Ethnic Studies Department at the University of California at Berkeley. It was in her class that I made my first film. From that point on, I started calling myself a filmmaker. It was because of that class that I saw film-making as an occupation and began the path of creating documentaries about social movements, music, and cultures around the world.

Arash: If you could share advice with any neophyte filmmakers attempting to do socially conscious work, what would it be?

Eli: You should start by asking yourself, 'Why do you want to make the film or tell that particular story?' The follow-up question to that is, 'Are you the right person to tell the story?' Many of us in the storytelling world are asking questions that generations before us did not ask. Some of the questions are, 'What does 'just' storytelling look like?' In other words, 'What does justice look like in the process of storytelling?' or 'What does extractive storytelling look like?' Oftentimes, we see the same scenario play out again and again; a white journalist or filmmaker comes to a community that has been historically oppressed and that community's story happens to be the talk of the country in that moment. They get some footage and return home, edit the piece, and then travel the country as experts about whatever subject the film is about.

It was very hard for me early on to find teachers, mentors and storytellers that had a practice of accountability to the people they told stories about. When you no longer have subjects or characters in your production, but rather contributors and collaborators, the entire dynamic changes. Early on I didn't have mentors to guide me or a tangible approach to what is now known as just filmmaking, my focus early on was about extractive practices to avoid. When we can't find people around us to emulate, the work relationships we create are open to *our* imagination. When you don't have a path to follow, you have the opportunity to create your own. So that's what I did. I created work relationships with the people in front of the camera and behind the camera that were authentic and based on mutual respect.

I believe that storytelling should be collaborative and created in partnership with the people whose experiences are being shared. A good question to ask yourself in creating a just storytelling project is, 'What communities are you a part of that need to be represented or represented better?' Many of my mentors in filmmaking started by telling their own stories. This is a great way to start because your life and your story is unique and at the same time you will, for the rest of your storytelling days, remember what it is like to be in front of the camera and how vulnerable that can feel. My hope is that, as a filmmaker, you would treat other stories with the same delicacy and care that you treat your own.

The best way to get better at anything in life is to do it often. Yes, studying the craft is important but get out there and tell stories. Find mentors and people with skills you don't have. Then find ways to work with and be around those that inspire you. With social media, you already have a built-in audience. Create work, share your work, get feedback, and create more.

Arash: I understand that you have made three movies about Cuba, "Inventos: HipHop Cubano," "Tengo Talento" and "Bakosó: Afrobeats of Cuba." What would you say are the primary similarities and differences? What compelled you to visit Cuba and compose works of art about it?

Eli: My big brother Kahlil, one half of our production team The Fantauzzi Brothers, invited me to travel to Cuba my senior year of college just after taking my first film class at UC Berkeley. He had already traveled to Cuba in 1994 to protest the US embargo. When he was there he met Cuban Hip Hop pioneers Amenaza who later became the group Orishas. As soon as I arrived in Cuba my brother picked me up from the airport and took me to a club near the malecon where Dead Prez was performing. The party was packed with people attending the International Hip-Hop Festival. I put my luggage behind the DJ booth and started filming.

As Hip Hop heads from two different countries, we all were excited to learn from one another. We became like family, and I was welcomed into their homes. Our relationships grew, and they trusted me with their stories as we shared experiences and our love for Hip Hop music and culture.

When I came back to the Bay Area with this footage, my friends were surprised to see Cuba portrayed so differently than what they see on the news. This encouraged me to continue filming and create a film. Inventos is a slang word they use in Cuba that means to create something out of nothing. This was reflected in my own journey, shooting the film on a digital-8 camera. This creativity in the face of limited resources is the foundation of Hip Hop.

The second film I directed in Cuba is called *Tengo Talento*, which is about emerging artists in Cuba. World renowned artists take to the streets to find the new generation of talent in their field. Many of my friends from the first film had left Cuba to pursue their dreams elsewhere. I wanted to explore the stories of famous artists who travel the world but choose to stay and live in Cuba. I wanted to see who they were mentoring and find out who were the next stars of Cuba. The film takes you on a journey from Havana to Santiago exploring Jazz, Hip Hop, Rumba, and more.

Bakosó: Afrobeats of Cuba was created when I returned back to Cuba after finishing my film HomeGrow: HipLife in Ghana. I showed the film to Dj Jigüe who is from Santiago De Cuba but was living in Havana at the time. After the film he told me that in Santiago they are creating a similar sound influenced by the African medical students at the Medical University of Santiago de Cuba. The music the African students brought with them was combined in the studio with the local rhythms of Santiago. We decided together to go back to his hometown and tell the story of this new genre being born. Bakosó: Afrobeats of Cuba is a reminder that our connection to Africa is not a thing of the past, the film shows what happens when Afrobeats hits Cuba.

Arash: How do you define activism? Do you consider yourself an activist? What does activism look like in your professional and personal life?

Eli: The word activism is played out. We live in a country where Chevron, one of the most detrimental polluters, funds one of the largest so-called environmental campaigns, with billboards and television commercials about saving trees. This is a country in which Phillip Morris, the owner of Marlboro, runs the highest and most well-known anti-tobacco campaigns; a country that is home to people who travel around the world taking selfies with some of the poorest communities—helping because they want to feel better about themselves and not because they seek to change the conditions their own lifestyles help perpetuate.

To me, activism means recognizing and valuing the humanity in other people and using my life, voice and resources to support others when that humanity is denied. Unfortunately, the term has been hijacked by for-profit, self-interested entities who have found ways to monetize it, making it difficult for me to associate with the term itself. But the sentiment is still there. It exists in my efforts to seek justice and fight against oppression: Uplifting our voices and our experiences and working in solidarity and honoring what it truly means to be an ally.

The choices we make every day, how we treat our neighbors, where we spend our money, what media we consume are just as or even more important than what protest we choose to attend. Every day I think about my position and my privilege. I look myself in the mirror, ask myself hard questions, check my ego, forgive myself and love myself, that is what activism accountability looks like to me.

Arash: What is the intersection of activism and Hip Hop? What was the moment when you first fell in love with the genre of Hip Hop?

Eli: I have always understood Hip Hop as a culture, not a genre. While there is no particular instance that I can point to and say 'this was the moment I fell in love with Hip Hop,' I do have some fond childhood memories of growing up with my older brother Kahlil and a number of other kids who I looked up to and being introduced to the culture through them. When they started B-Boying [breakdancing], I followed suit. We would get together and practice our moves on cardboard boxes. I also distinctly remember talking my mother, Lila, into taking my brother and I to a Grandmaster Flash and the Furious Five concert. My mother was a PhD student at the University of Santa Barbara at the time, so my request was pretty far-fetched, but she must have seen the excitement in my eyes. That night, I was mesmerized by Melle Mel's skills on the mic and his wild outfit. That was a night I definitely remember falling in love with the movement I already started to feel a part of.

Arash: I understand that your father is a musician and your mother an educator and a light show artist, what role did they play in shaping your work and Hip Hop activism?

Eli: I am the product of a draft-dodging musician and an expatriate lightshow artist. My parents chose those routes because they believed in creating a better world and they raised and encouraged me to find my own path. I believe the best way to have a more loving, just, and compassionate society is through storytelling. That is why I became a filmmaker. I travel the world looking to be inspired, moved, and challenged to become my best self. The stories I find, or those that sometimes find me, manifest themselves in my films, my art and my personal artistic expressions.

One of my greatest missions in life is to amplify the voices of people who refuse to be silenced, ignored, and cut off from the larger society. My dedication to visual art is deeply connected to my commitment to social justice and the belief in the transformative power of storytelling. I have always been attracted to stories that explore and promote healing. The field of documentary filmmaking has created a name for itself by telling devastating stories of pain and tragedy that often leave the viewer broken-hearted, overwhelmed and sad. Those stories surely have their place, but I am invested in making room for uplifting stories that show ingenuity and strength in the face of adversity; films full of music and culture that leave viewers feeling empowered and believing they can become change agents in their personal lives, their communities, and the world.

Whether I am teaching Race and Ethnicity in Contemporary American Film at UC Berkeley or presenting my work at the Zanzibar International Film Festival, I remind the audience that it is our duty to build something powerful, useful, and innovative out of what seems impossible or lacking in value. Poor and disenfranchised communities around the world don't have the same access to tell their own stories. Mainstream media has monopolized what stories get told and who gets to tell them. As the age-old African proverb goes, "until the lion tells his side of the story, the tale of the hunt will always glorify the hunter." I use the platforms I have created to tell the lion's story.

Arash: What do you believe are the most salient connections between Hip Hop and social activism?

Eli: Hip Hop is the voice of oppressed and marginalized communities in the United States and around the world. When we talk about justice and equity, we're talking about listening to the voices and stories of communities around us that are the most cut off from society and the inception of Hip Hop was exactly that. It created space for marginalized and oppressed people around the world that needed an avenue for their voices and experiences to be heard.

Now that Hip Hop has been around for decades and we've experienced the commercialization of Hip Hop, we are now seeing how the foundational culture has kept it alive and thriving. No longer limited to just the five elements, the full aesthetic of Hip Hop, what it means historically, and how it came to be has influenced people in every industry.

To me, Hip Hop and social activism means hearing from the people that are most affected by systems of inequality, and recognizing them as experts of their own experience. Sometimes the best-intentioned activists enter communities, and instead of amplifying the voices of those communities, they end up imposing their own visions, values and voices. What Hip Hop has taught me is that the role of the activist is to uplift the voices of marginalized people and create spaces for those voices to be heard.

For example, Hip Hop as an educational tool means creating a paradigm shift in which teachers become the students because they recognize youth are living and creating the culture, every day. This role-reversal allows for youth to speak from a place of power and knowledge. This paradigm shift is the essence of Hip Hop. As an aesthetic, Hip Hop is about who's in control, who has the power, and who has the voice; who's telling the story?

Arash: Your work covering young people expressing themselves in Hip Hop has also taken you to Ghana and Colombia. Could you talk a bit about your artistic work in those nations?

Eli: My films in both Ghana and Medellin, Colombia are both about young people finding ways to express themselves through Hip Hop. For almost two decades, Hip Hop has merged with High-Life, the traditional music of West Africa, and this fusion has led to a new musical genre called HipLife. It is what opened the door for the massive Afrobeat explosion today.

My film, *HomeGrown: HipLife in Ghana*, documents 10 years with the group Vision In Progress (VIP) as they journey from what they call the ghetto in Accra, to their first international tour. They grow from being teenagers with a shared dream to musicians with fans around the world. Before I even started filming for this project I lived in Ghana for over a year and was a part of the Study Abroad program at the University of Legon. I hosted a radio show at "Radio Universe 105.7", the school's station. It was there that I first was introduced to the local Ghanian rap scene.

My time in Ghana changed my life forever. Because everything was so new to me, I felt like my entire life was put under a microscope. I asked myself hard questions about my identity. Why did I wear baggy jeans and sag my pants? At home I had an answer, I was rebelling against a system and government that I felt was unjust and racist. But that answer did not work in Ghana, I was under a different system of beliefs and in an entirely different society so why would I rebel in the same ways? My entire life my identity had been built around what I was against, living in Ghana was the first time I asked myself what I stood for and how I could represent that in the way I showed up in the world. So, when I met the Hip Hop crew in Accra and I saw them in their baggy clothes and do-rags, I knew they were rebelling but in a different context. Again this was an opportunity for me to learn about new customs in a new country through our shared love for Hip Hop culture.

Years after my time in Ghana, I was presenting my work about Hip Hop around the world at a university on the East Coast. When I showed a music video I shot in Colombia with Chocquibtown, one of the students got very excited because he was from there. After the class, we talked about our time in Colombia and he told me he wanted to help me produce a documentary there. We were soon travelling to Comuna 13 in Medellin—a battleground between military police and different armed neo-paramilitary groups. Fighting over control in the different neighborhoods resulted in a staggering nine people murdered every day. The youth living in this area are often recruited as a part of the war or tragically caught in the crossfire, but the tide is changing and many have chosen to fight back peacefully. Today, there are dozens of community organizations created and administered by teenagers using Hip Hop as a strategy to empower themselves and change not only their lives but the lives of those around them.

This turned into a film project called *Revolución Sin Muertos* (A Revolution Without Death) that went inside this inspiring non-violent revolution by following organizers from La Elite and Son Bata, two youth organizations desperately trying to save the lives of their community and sometimes even their own family.

Arash: For many scholar activists, pushing the boundaries of historical imperialism, the academy has been a source of pushback and social reproduction. What are the greatest challenges you face when promoting your work within the academy? What advice do you give to others attempting to surmount the same hurdles within the academy, if any?

Eli: After graduating from UC Berkeley, I had the opportunity to teach the next generation of filmmakers at Berkeley High School how to create their own films. When I realized that my students were surpassing my own skills, I made the decision to go back to school. After six years of teaching, I moved to the East Coast and enrolled into NYU's Tisch School of the Arts. I obtained a Master's Degree in a program dedicated to interactive art called Interactive Telecommunications Program (ITP). Not only did a formal education help me hone my skills and learn my craft, but it also gave me credentials from prestigious universities that have undoubtedly opened many doors for me that I may have had to pry open under different circumstances. One such opportunity was teaching a class at UC Berkeley called *Race and Ethnicity in Contemporary American Film*. Being able to break the films down and discuss them in a college setting was a great opportunity.

While my degrees have certainly opened doors, it is also true that my decision to leave academia in the pursuit of a career as an independent filmmaker has left many doors closed to me. I often feel like I am straddling both worlds as someone who was educated by some of the most prestigious institutions, but who has chosen a path that does not depend on the academy for acknowledgement and support, yet still welcomes opportunities, such as lecturing and showing my films, when I am offered. In many ways, I have accepted this status as a filmmaker who is not fully integrated into the academy and whose work, for the most part, exists outside of the academy. Because of this intentional choice and positionality, my relationship to the academy is not necessarily adversarial and certainly not a perspective of someone who is struggling to surmount hurdles.

In fact, I find tremendous value in travel and the continuous learning and growth that visiting other places and experiencing other cultures can offer that an ivory tower cannot. I have grown so much as both a filmmaker and individual from my experiences and from what I've seen traveling the world, and I recognize my privilege and understand that a lot of people don't have that opportunity. Making these films is a way to bring some of that back with me to share with my community so they can see and learn from my experiences.

It's when you travel outside of your own culture that you realize how much of that culture you emulate; like a fish that doesn't know it's in water until you take it out. When you look at yourself on film, you get a similar experience. Whether I was documenting Hip Hop in Cuba, HipLife in Ghana or the youth creating a peace movement in Colombia, each of those communities were able to look at themselves on the big screen for the first time and reflect back about the impact their work has had.

Arash: Where has the natural arc of your artistic and scholarly work taken you now? What is your next project and why?

Eli: I am currently dedicated to a project called Defend Puerto Rico (Defend PR). The Defend PR project—based in Puerto Rico—started as a way for me, a member of the diaspora, to establish and maintain a meaningful connection to the island. At the time of Defend PR's inception, I was living in California and after hearing a lot of alarming statistics regarding the island's debt crisis and about people leaving the island, en masse, I felt compelled to travel to the island to Borikén to see for myself what was actually happening. When I returned home to California, having had this transformational experience, I felt deeply that other people, members of the diaspora and our allies, should have access to the stories and information I was able to learn first-hand. Defend PR was born out of this desire. I started the project with a core team of other Puerto Rican artists, social entrepreneurs, media producers, and change makers in an effort to cultivate meaningful dialogue about the social issues and struggles affecting Puerto Ricans on the island, and create a reliable information hub for others interested in learning about and supporting Puerto Ricans working for social transformation.

Defend PR's vision is to use our interactive, multi-media platform to amplify the voices of everyday Puerto Ricans working to build a new Puerto Rico where its land, people, and culture flourish. By using a people-centered approach to storytelling and the dissemination of personal and community narratives, we aspire to capture the remarkable resilience and creativity of the Puerto Rican people as they navigate the current economic and fiscal crisis. We share stories of resistance and renewal in all areas of Puerto Rican society and cultural life, highlighting everything from agriculture and cultural production, to grassroots political mobilization and global solidarity networks.

While the Defend PR mission has not changed post Hurricane Maria, my role and relation to the island has. Post Maria, I put down the camera for a bit in order to help rebuild the town of Comerío that was devastated by the hurricane. Initially working to get food and water to people without access and addressing other immediate needs, to later painting houses, removing debris and clearing homes of furniture and personal items left rotted and molded by rain and flood waters, and later rebuilding roofs and entire homes. After teaching photography and video to the youth in Comerío, I picked the camera back up and together we created the film "We Still Here." A documentary film that shows the youth taking control of rebuilding efforts post Hurricane Maria and transforming their lives as well as their community.

You can tune into ongoing updates from that project at www.westillherepr.com

Arash: How can the public follow your work as someone who seeks justice through filmmaking?

Eli: @FistupTV twitter and Instagram

www.FistUp.tv

CHAPTER THREE

Interview with "Mic" Crenshaw

ANTHONY J. NOCELLA II

Anthony: Tell me your story on how you got involved in the Hip Hop community and some of your first memorable moments when you joined the Hip Hop community on an active level?

"Mic": In 1980, I was living in Springfield, Illinois and going back and forth between there and my hometown of Chicago. I remember the first time I heard "Rapper's Delight" (Sugar Hill Gang), I was at The Boys Club in the projects in Springfield. Shortly thereafter I heard "The Message" by Grandmaster Flash and the Furious 5 while on Summer Break in Chicago. Prior to hearing these songs, I had only liked hard rock and some of the pop and soul music my parents and relatives listened to. Rap music was new to my ears but familiar to my soul. As a ten-year-old boy struggling with issues of race and identity, this music was empowering to me and I was immediately drawn to it and intrigued by it. I wouldn't be long before I would emulate it, teaching myself how to freestyle rap.

As a teenager and into my early twenties in Minneapolis, Minnesota, I was part of the hardcore punk scene and intimately involved in the anti-racist movement as a founding member of the Minneapolis Baldies. The Baldies were ethnically mixed and even though we were anti-racist skinheads, many of us also loved Hip Hop music and culture and were taggers, graffiti writers and B-boys. I was from Chicago originally and lived on the Northside of MPLS and I had friends and cousins, classmates who were part of Hip Hop crews. At a certain point, the Baldies decided to strategically build alliances with King's Posse and Mental Madness Posse which were Hip Hop Cultural organizations that had heavy membership from Black and Latino youth, many of whom were also gang members in different *Folks* and *Peoples* gangs. *Folks* and *Peoples* Nations were rival factions built from numerous gangs originally from Chicago. We partied together and fought Nazi's together and would wind up at Ice-T and Public Enemy shows. One memorable night back in 1987, we all got together and filled multiple vehicles, about 40 of us. We drove to St. Paul to confront White Supremacists at a concert.

The youth culture in the streets of Minneapolis at that time was one heavily influenced by Hip Hop. Rap music, graffiti writing and the more subtle elements of self assuredness, resilience and strength in numbers were traits that we identified with overtly and internally.

As a form of entertainment, we used to freestyle rhyme in cyphers and "play the dozens" through rhyme verses. Battles between the most skilled emcees would happen on the back of the bus and in school hallways and classrooms.

When I moved to Portland in the early 1990's, I took my love of Hip Hop seriously enough to start rapping locally and doing spoken word at poetry slams. I won my first battle here in Portland on KBOO Community Radio and have since been a leader as an artist, educator and organizer in the scene.

Anthony: What does Hip Hop mean to you and can you provide a few examples of how Hip Hop has challenged, changed, and overall influenced society, globally?

"Mic": For me, Hip Hop had taught me how to love my most authentic self and respect others who exhibit similar traits. The competitive elements of Hip Hop culture encouraged me to develop a style that I believed to be unique. I believe there have always been ways of borrowing and sampling other people's characteristics that are undeniably effective and a dope way that our culture grows and expands and maintains an ability to be recognized. I also know that the most respected expressions in our culture, though they may borrow elements from individuals and groups from outside and within the Hip Hop genre, the most respected characteristic is originality. Borrow, but make it fly and own it as your own creation; improve upon what you have.

When I travel globally to Africa, Europe, Asia and Latin America, I see how Hip Hop means just as much or more to people from all over the world. In many places where there is poverty and a lack of access to wealth, people are living Hip Hop in its highest expressions through music, dance, visual art and connection to political consciousness inspired by Black History and Anti-Colonial struggles.

I was invited by Hip Hop cultural activists from Zimbabwe, and South Africa to participate in an international Hip Hop project called the Afrikan Hip Hop Caravan in 2012. Since then I have been invited to Tanzania, Cuba, Germany, Kenya and back to South Africa and Zimbabwe numerous times to perform and participate as an organizer in events, festivals, and tours. The majority of the artists I am connected to in the aforementioned countries are artists as well as activists and educators who are committed to human rights and justice, youth empowerment and popular education in their respective communities. The participants in the Afrikan Hip Hop Caravan often say that Hip Hop stands for His or Her Infinite Power Helping Oppressed People.

In my observation of and participation in the culture of Hip Hop, I am aware of the way that street slang makes it into mainstream culture. I often notice the terms we use in regular day to day conversations have been brought to us by Hip Hop. The presence of Hip Hop aesthetics in fashion, marketing and branding, in sports and entertainment as a whole is pervasive. Even though many elements of capitalist consumer culture extracts, steals and borrows from Hip Hop, I do not choose to look at this as solely a negative thing. The power that cultures of resistance can have to influence dominant culture is what is most important to recognize and remember. The power comes from the people, not from exploitation.

Anthony: While many believe Hip Hop is political, very few identify themselves as a Hip Hop activist. Can you explain what Hip Hop activism is and is not and give examples of it? Who are key individuals that should be noted as key founders and mentors of Hip Hop activism and why?

"Mic": When I got started in anti-racist organizing as a founding member of ARA and the *MPLS Baldies* in about 1986, I was doing so because my friends and I as teenagers felt a sense of responsibility. We had already learned that those in authority were at best apathetic and at worst corrupt and in collusion with the enemy in the interest of white supremacy. I had experienced police brutality numerous times at the hands of racist cops. I had read about the Black Power Movement and began to see the way the Gang Task Force were targeting and harassing us was reminiscent of COINTELPRO. I took notice of how the violent Klan and neo-Nazis were often protected by police at public marches and demonstrations. I was starting to read and attend study groups. The political education I got as time went on was the result of doing the work and that allowed elders to take notice and intervene. Some played a crucial role in my mentorship and development of my political consciousness. I was able to see that the work I was being moved to do in defense of my rights as a Black human in a white supremacist society was connected to older movements for liberation and self-determination.

The lyrics of Ice Cube, Chuck D., X-Clan, KRS One, Brand Nubian, Paris and others began to mirror what I was going through in my own consciousness and development. The elders were exposing me to information about the Black Panthers and other freedom fighters. I read Assata Shakur and I was inspired to join the struggle. My identity was beginning to come into its own and it was the activism that grounded me in a purpose beyond my own egotistical desires for pleasure, escapism, and notoriety as a young man in the streets.

While attending high school in Minneapolis, Cheri Honkala was instrumental in recruiting me into the Poor Peoples' Movement and I began to go on speaking tours and attend conferences across the Midwest and on the East Coast where I spoke on panels and debated with other activists. Nelson Peery and the Communist Labor Party were critical in my understanding of capitalism as a root cause of oppression. This was in the late 80's and 90's.

In 1994, I was invited to front a band as an emcee here in Portland, Oregon. I named the band Hungry Mob after lyrics spit by Bob Marley in "Dem Belly Full." We quickly became a popular band in the region and my lyricism as an emcee became a channel for my political consciousness. By the time I saw Dead Prez on MTV, in the early 2000's I was further determined to remain a political rapper and Hip Hop activist.

Rosa Clemente, Jared A. Ball, Davey D, Shamako Noble through Hip Hop Congress, Immortal Technique through music, Dead Prez through music and collaboration, Boots Riley, Rebel Diaz, Homeboy Sandman, Mama C and Pete O'Neal, and many lesser known activists from the *Soundz Of The South Collective* in South Africa, the Uhuru Network in Zimbabwe and SUA in Tanzania have had a major influence on me.

On a recent trip to Tanzania, I invited Daniel Lasuncet, a 1st year college student who is a music producer, singer, and an emcee to accompany me. I wanted to introduce him to some of the people and experiences made available to me through the *Afrikan Hip Hop Caravan*. This was Daniel's first time outside of the US and in Africa. While in Tanzania, we took a day trip to Ngorongoro Crater, a national park and wildlife sanctuary. On the way back our vehicle broke down and we had to stop in small town to have it repaired. While the truck was being worked on, Daniel and I took a walk and we were almost immediately surrounded by young people who could tell we were from the US and were curious about who we were. This happens often while I'm traveling in Africa. I sensed that Daniel was nervous and contemplating ways to respond and interact with these assertive strangers. I suggested he lead with Hip Hop and let this particular group of six to ten young men know that he was an emcee and beat maker. Once he did, the connection was immediate and almost overwhelming. Every one of them grew even more excited, pulled out their phones and began playing local artists and beats, and some started rapping themselves. Contact information was exchanged and Daniel and I, as well as the locals now understood that we were all part of a global phenomenon that we each had stake in. That's the power of Hip Hop.

Anthony: What issues, tactics, and strategies make Hip Hop activism different than other forms of activism such as feminism, LGBTTQQIA, disability activism, animal rights activism, environmentalism, social justice activism, anti-war activism, vegan activism, food justice, environmental justice, transgender activism, transnational feminism, and decolonizing activism?

"Mic": To me in the U.S, and I think many places in the African Diaspora and across the continent of Africa, many of us understand that at its root, Hip Hop is an African cultural form of expression that comes out of the current and historical realities of Black Peoples' experiences on Earth. So with Hip Hop and all that comes from it, there is something at its root that is understood as explicitly Black. I recognize that people from all cultures and ethnicities, races and religions, gender identities participate and contribute to the ongoing development of Hip Hop, but in my mind, what separates our culture in history, substance, content and form, is its Blackness. Often this aspect is debated about, forgotten, denied, overlooked, misunderstood, but it remains something that is not present in such a fundamental way in other forms of activism, expression, activity that is not Hip Hop in origin. Many of the other forms of political activism, at least here and in other places, like Europe, are dominated by whiteness. In many other spheres of political activism, identity politics and mass movement, Blackness is marginalized, excluded, policed, feared, not honored, respected or centered.

Questions of gender identity, sexism, oppression against femmes, sexual violence, and misogyny often get lumped together when we examine them as if from an outside position of relative privilege. Though there are intersections and the root causes are from a common source, all of these things are not the same. We all experience oppression very subjectively even though we know that the objective fact is that we are all targets of oppression. Its complex because as a Black person, and as a cisgender heterosexual man I have a worldview that has been shaped by how dominant culture defines me, allows me access to relative privilege and assigns identity to me. I am also self-aware and self-determined to establish my own identity in opposition to systems of oppression. In me responding to historic, systemic oppression and violence against my being I can see both a defensive reaction to any critique of the cultures I self-identify with as well as an opportunity for growth and reflection. When people say, "Hip Hop is misogynous," I will get defensive and want to have a deeper critical discussion of why that is a dangerous generalization. I have to be willing to speak up for the revolutionary and liberatory examples available and thriving in hip hop as a culture beyond the genre of music, but I also have to know that it is not my role to make invisible or take space from non—men who need to speak their own truths about what it means to be in this culture in the bodies that they are in.

We have a long way to go in Hip Hop Culture to continue to honor and respect people, ideas and spaces that are not overtly, ableist, heteronormative, patriarchal, environmentally conscious, oppressive and exploitative to women. I do see that work happening and there have always been people who are radical enough in their consciousness and approach to look at intersectionality and push for a more inclusive cultural reality in Hip Hop. I do feel that some of us in this culture know and understand that as members of an historically and currently oppressed people, that we must be committed to ending oppression for all people and all life on Earth.

Being an activist for most of my life means that I have been in thousands of meetings doing organizing work, building coalitions, reading, studying, and debating. None of this work promises to be fun or even inspiring and a lot of it is mundane, taxing and will burn you out. Hip Hop allows us to bring a cultural element that is full of expression, reflection, life, light, power and beauty. The rhythm of the lyrics can make the message memorable. The music and dance, the participatory nature of Hip Hop, the reciprocity between the call of the performer and the response of the audience breaks the monotony and adds character to our movements that can actually instill joy in our work.

Anthony: How long have you been doing Hip Hop activism and in what ways have you engaged in Hip Hop activism? Can you tell us some successful Hip Hop activist events you have organized and participated in and why they were successful in your opinion?

"Mic": I have been a Hip Hop activist for over 30 years. I first began as a teenager in Minneapolis, Minnesota, building unity among youth subcultures to combat violent white supremacist gangs. The demographics of my organizing base were left wing working class white kids and youth from the Black, Latinx, Native and Asian-American Communities. Many of these kids were Hip Hop 'heads' and would go on to become professional artists within the Hip Hop industry.

There were a series of Youth Summits and Poor Peoples' Movement conferences in the 90's in Minneapolis and Chicago that I helped play a role in organizing, mobilizing and leading workshops in.

In Portland, Oregon in 1994, I began organizing in the Hip Hop Community as an emcee and band member in Hungry Mob. Together with many of the city's veteran Hip Hop artists we founded POHHOP, the Portland, Oregon Hip Hop Festival. The festival featured over 30 local acts and went on for close to a decade as an annual event drawing sold out crowds, producing compilation records and collaborations and a sense of solidarity in the city amongst Hip Hop artists.

Using my skills as a performer, organizer, and educator, I have been a teaching artist for most of my life, utilizing Hip Hop and spoken word as a means to engage students with social-justice issues.

Going into high schools with peace activists and informing educators and activists about the tactics of military recruiters in targeting low-income students for recruitment is the work that got me invited to a conference on economic justice, youth empowerment, HIV/AIDS and genocide reconciliation in Rwanda in 2004. The conditions of my participation on this trip were that I follow up with two years of service work related to the project. While in Rwanda I was asked by a group of activists to help start a computer center to educate youth in the region. When I got back to the U.S, I reached out to Dead Prez and asked for their support in the effort. Dead Prez played at a show organized by Global Fam an LLC working with a non-profit called Education Without Borders.

Together we raised enough money to ship donated computers to Bujumbura, Burundi and establish a computer center that we still support today. They have helped teach hundreds of youth computer literacy skills and be better equipped for employment and further education.

The work I did with Global Fam, with activists in Africa and the computer center reverberated and I was invited to return to Africa in 2012 to play at the Shoko Festival in Zimbabwe. At Shoko, I was invited to become a Lead Organizer in the U.S for the *Afrikan Hip Hop Caravan*, a grassroots international Hip Hop project organized by Hip Hop collectives in multiple countries in Africa. I toured and organized with the Caravan in multiple cities in South Africa, Tanzania, Zimbabwe and Kenya in 2013, 2014, and 2015.

In 2015 I took a high school student with me on tour with the Caravan to Tanzania, Kenya, Zimbabwe and South Africa and in 2018, I took a first year college student majoring in music with me to Tanzania. Both of these students are Hip Hop artists. I am committed to making the greatest opportunities that I have had access to available to youth who are coming up behind me.

I will continue to develop an international cultural exchange through the vector of Hip Hop and provide opportunities for individuals and groups to explore the possibilities for global exchange through actual collaborative projects. We have successfully built and supported two computer centers in Burundi through my company *Global Fam*. We will continue to collaborate with the United African Alliance Community Center in Tanzania. UAACC was founded by Pete and Charlotte O'Neal, two Black Panthers in political exile, living in Africa since the 1970's. Their lifelong commitment to community service is in alignment with their identity as Black Panther Party members. To me, being able to work with these political giants as my mentors and to get their support consistently is beyond priceless. It is a direct link to the work of those that came before me and exists as a powerful continuum through the work I do currently and into the foreseeable future.

Anthony: In what ways do you see Hip Hop activism growing and being needed in society and within the realm of Hip Hop? What are some campaigns that Hip Hop activists are pushing and working on right now and should be working on now or in the future?

"Mic": I am currently a Teaching Artist in Residence at an alternative high school. I have been teaching social justice and history through an anti—oppression lens and using Hip Hop to do so for close to 30 years. In that time, I have engaged thousands of young people as audience members, students, fans. One of the most remarkable things that I can see is how knowledge is passed on from one generation to the next. The concept of each one teach one. There have often been times when I'm in the community or on social media that a younger person will approach me and communicate to me that I was an inspiration to them and that I played a crucial role in their development. I am always humbled and moved by this experience when it happens. It's the memories of this happening that help me to stay committed to my craft as an artist and as an educator and activist who serves my community locally and globally.

I began writing poetry and rap songs that expressed the thoughts, feelings and ideas that I wanted to see a reflection of in art. I am going to continue working to inspire others to do the same.

When the forces that drive the commodification and marketing of our cultural products are in alignment with the destruction of our lives, we have to respond in a way that doesn't reinforce our destruction. Our cultural expression can be a means through which we preserve the best parts of our ancestral heritage and the victories that were won through struggles for freedom.

Even though business interests will continue to exploit human and natural resources to the point of extinction, we can resist, fight and create alternative realities that no longer rely on the paradigm that was created to destroy us. We will continue to do this through Hip Hop.

Hip Hop comes from the voices and expressions of the marginalized and oppressed. As long as economic and social conditions exist in a dynamic that benefits the few at the expense of the masses, Hip Hop culture will have a home in the slums, ghettos, reservations and townships globally. What started as a youth culture will continue to produce lifelong adherents and creative people who will remain Hip Hop into their elder years. The multi-generational existence of this global culture will continue to gather attention and fans and achieve commercial success, creating jobs for artists, designers, managers, agents, academics and numerous other fields. Parents and grandparents who are professional Hip Hop artists and experts in one or more of the traditional elements will raise their children to be "Hip Hoppers". Academics and scholars are already teaching Hip Hop history and using rap songs from 2Pac and others as teaching tools.

Health and wellness has become the 10th Element of Hip Hop culture thanks to artists including, Dead Prez, Keith Tucker and others. Words like sustainability, inclusion and equity are words that resonate with people who come from frontline communities where poverty, disease, violence and environmental racism are rampant. We need to make sure these words aren't just token phrases meant to attract funders to short lived non-profit hustles, but that the language informs practices that become part of our daily lives.

Political campaigns, in an effort to reach young voters and seem relevant, use Hip Hop as a means of validating and branding their image. This will continue. Hip Hop education and teaching artists will continue to have a presence in schools and universities.

In the interest of immigrant rights, healthcare for all, an end to the prison industrial complex and the military industrial complex, and destruction of our natural world and other species, Hip Hop has a proverbial voice.

As humanity begins to grapple with our own collective mortality as a race amidst escalating ecological, environmental, economic, health and military crises, the minds of *Hip Hoppers* will be at the table thinking critically about solutions to the problems we face in our world.

CHAPTER FOUR

Interview with Reies Romero

ANTHONY J. NOCELLA II

Anthony: Can you detail your story on how you got involved in the Hip Hop community, and if you could, tell us about some of the first memorable moments of when you became active in this community?

Reies: Born to a Chicano father and a mother of European descent in Albuquerque, New Mexico in May of 1976, I grew up in the Twin Cities of Minnesota. I fell in love with Hip Hop culture at a very young age, initially attracted to the dance form of Hip Hop that is referred to as B-boying or later on, breakin'. I would practice every day and my attachment to the art form grew immensely as a young kid. I would listen to groups such as Grandmaster Flash and the Furious Five, U.T.F.O, Roxanne Shante, Mantronix, Kurtis Blow, Nucleus, Run-DMC, Too Short, Public Enemy, N.W.A., OutKast, The Geto Boys, Big Daddy Kane, The Fat Boys, DJ Quick, MC Lyte, De La, Tribe, Pete Rock & C.L. Smooth, Heavy D, Common and countless others. These artists changed my life for the better and shaped my thinking, my attitude, my style of dress, my language and outlook on life. As I grew into my teen years, I started to collect a few records here and there and at age 12, I attended my first real Hip Hop show, "The 2 Live Crew." They were playing a show at the Varsity Theater in Dinkytown (circa '91). I remember it vividly; the local openers, the energy, the DJ (Mister Mix) and all my friends from school that were present. This concert was one of my fondest memories.

Fast forward a few years, I attended a concert at the Orpheum Theater in downtown Minneapolis which featured Chubb Rock, Redhead Kingpin and Apache (RIP). This is where I witnessed one of the dopest DJ routines I have ever seen to this day. Apache's DJ, whose name I forgot, but he did his infamous cereal bowl trick while juggling "It Takes Two" by Rob Base & DJ EZ Rock. I was in complete amazement and this was the night I decided I wanted to pursue becoming a DJ. I was highly influenced by local legends DJ Disco T and Dan Speak. They would throw these parties like none I have ever seen since in and around the Twin Cities. I would sit and watch Disco T's every move and study how he cleverly read the crowd.

Twenty-five years later I am still a proud DJ and beholder of DJ culture, ethics and principles. I was that kid walking around with a piece of cardboard ready to dance, battle, and express myself. During high school, I would practice DJing every day after school with my friend Fernando Aguilar. We would play records for hours on end, well until my mother yelled at me to turn it off! I would build my record collection any time I had money to spare; record shopping was like a weekend ritual, smoke some broccoli [marijuana] and go record shopping for the new shit that would come out. I would sneak into and steal from my mother's record collection before I could afford to buy vinyl on my own. I got with a crew because it is the natural essence of Hip Hop culture. One does not practice the culture alone; it is a communal effort, it is a community in progress and in action. One of my first crews was the *612 Crew*. We would have freestyle sessions in my bedroom while I played records. Later I joined RhymeSayers Entertainment. Siddiq and I became close and he would take me with him to DJ whenever RSE, or its affiliates at the time, had shows and/or functions. This created a path for me and I joined RSE's Los Nativos, which was known as the Native Ones back then (circa '97). I was a resident DJ at First Avenue Nightclub for nearly six years where I DJ'ed countless shows, conducted my own DJ Night called "The Barbershop" with my co-DJ partners Cornelius and Henry Mhoon, joined a crew called SPStyle and the Department Appointed Public Officials (D.A.P.O), aka the Hip Hop Protection Force. This led me all the way to the Twin Cites Omega Zuluz (Zulu Union) and the James Dewitt Yancey Foundation. It has been a long ride and I stay busy promoting the elements of Hip Hop, youth empowerment and living by the Hip Hop principles of Peace, Love, Integrity and Work.

Anthony: What does Hip Hop mean to you and can you provide a few examples of how Hip Hop has challenged, changed, and influenced society as a whole, globally?

Reies: Hip Hop culture lives in my heart. It is part of who I am, just as my eyes, ears, and limbs are a part of my whole body. Hip Hop is part of my very existence and essence. It is the essence of my positionality in this world and one of my lenses of expression. Hip Hop is that feeling I get to stand up, to fight back against oppression, to establish justice wherever I am, to connect with others, to simply be me in all situations and to create equality through the fundamental principles of Hip Hop and its elements. Hip Hop is Peace, Love, Integrity, and Work. It is a driving energy and force that can never be stopped, well at least not 'til the world ends? There isn't an area on the globe that Hip Hop hasn't touched. Look at places like Asia, Afrika, Russia; Hip Hop has had an influence everywhere and it is not contained by any means. It may be suppressed or viewed as a threat, abstract or whatever, but it can never be eradicated or caged. Hip Hop has literally changed the world. It has changed the consciousness of millions of young people, middle-aged, and those of mature status. Hip Hop breathes life into the hearts of so many. It is powerful, beautiful, exciting, thought provoking and will always evolve. Hip Hop still challenges the status quo, even in our current educational system. It can be implemented to improve learning, especially for youth of color who are eternally bound to Hip Hop's white arbitrators and collectors, especially here in Minnesota, don't understand how Hip Hop reaches realms of learning and sparks parts of the brain and body that are necessary for learning. Take yoga for instance; yes, it is used in schools to center students, but Hip Hop can be used in the same way to direct a shift to focus, have fun, and learn new things through the art form of Hip Hop.

Anthony: While many believe Hip Hop is political, very few identify themselves as a Hip Hop Activist. Can you explain what Hip Hop activism is and is not, and give examples of it? Who are key individuals that should be noted as key founders and mentors of Hip Hop activism and why?

Reies: Hip Hop activism ultimately speaks through the artist and their music. I think about Chuck D with his relentless and revolutionary lyrics. I think of Rakim and his scientific approach at lyricism; Jeru the Damaja with his rough delivery, but positive message; Queen Latifah and her fight for gender empowerment; X-Clan with Afrocentric mind thought; Jean Grae with provoking rhymes; DJ Q-bert with his scratch techniques; Pop Master Fable still touching dance floors around the globe; Kid Frost with Brown Pride and Clear Soul Forces bringing fresh life to the culture. J Dilla is the best to ever produce. Others such as b-boy J-Sun with his Hip Hop pedagogy through the art of dance, Los Nativos with decolonizing Indigenous minds, and quoting Brother Ali:

Know that I'm a soldier, heart's on my battleground ...

Ain't worry bout ya threatening me, I'm just being honest

I ain't buying fear just because it's all you got left. (Ali, Own Light, 2017)

Hip Hop implies action. It is a word that demands knowledge with action, and there is no way around it, no way to sugar coat it or decrease the true meaning. Hip Hop activism is not just simply sharing already established ideas on social media, it is continuing to evolve, inserting fresh techniques and strategies to combat all forms of oppression. Evolving does not mean going backwards or the dumbing down of skill levels associated with the culture. I don't think I have ever heard so much "clone music" and biting as I have in the last 5–10 years. Hip Hop has resembled pop music more than it ever has before. Corporate entities have their dirty hands in practically everything. The youth nowadays listen to stuff that is devastating to their minds in ways they might not even understand. As a Hip Hop activist, I must tap into the youth's energy and meet them where they are at according to their specific experience with Hip Hop. Some youth say they could care less about lyrics, they just "feel the beat." Others are very lyrically conscious and search for quality in everything. It really just depends on who you talk with.

Hip Hop activism is connecting with the youth, connecting to that universal energy and fire in them. I had it, the generation before me had it; it's the same energy recycled. Tapping into it is the key to channeling that energy in a positive manner and movement. After all, Hip Hop is movement, it is the intimate connection between the dancer(s) and the DJ; that spark of energy, and the cosmic connection of beat and body. There's no doubt that Hip Hop is simultaneously a form of healing and resistance, the very core of its essence is deep inside, something undescribed and untouched.

Anthony: What issues, tactics, and strategies make Hip Hop activism different than other forms of activism such as feminism, LGBTTQQIA, disability activism, animal rights activism, environmentalism, social justice activism, anti-war activism, vegan activism, food justice, environmental justice, transgender activism, transnational feminism, and decolonizing activism?

Reies: Ultimately, Hip Hop activism encompasses many of the elements I mentioned above. Hip Hop came from the streets. There is knowledge in the streets if one searches for it. Sometimes it comes to you, but for the most part, the youth, the people have to be hungry to learn. Stomach hunger, shelter hunger, the pigs can overshadow this hunger for knowledge and the will of survival takes over. Many so-called Hip Hop artists are simply not cut out for Hip Hop activism, nor interested in participating in it. They simply don't care for the culture. Their focus is not liberation or empowerment and in many ways they inadvertently assist white supremacy by their narratives. The "out-for-self" narrative is so strong for many that improvement of one's people or community is a non-factor. So what do we do as Hip Hop activists?

First, we need to hold artists accountable; conscious artists need to hold other artists accountable. I mean, who cares if I say it? Who am I, right? It needs to be a level playing field when it comes to artists holding artists accountable. Years ago, people would call on Minister Farrakhan to settle disputes. Now there are so many "woke" thinkers, it is difficult to have viable opinions when so many are supporters of one but not the other. Take Umar Johnson's supporters and his opposition—who's right? How does the community decide? Everyone is going to have opposition, even me. Some in my own Twin Cities community don't agree with me. Some have even threatened me with physical harm, but do I let this stop me? Hell no! I channel that energy to motivate, inspire, and push me to do more every day. Hip Hop activism addresses such a wide range of issues, it is very complex. Hip Hop is rooted in struggle and the fight for liberation. The added activism is fairly new, but it makes sense now as it did in previous decades. This title of Hip Hop Activist is not to be taken lightly and should be taken seriously. On a recent trip to Seattle, I was granted Kingship under the sanction of the Zulu Union (est. 2017). I was overwhelmed to say the least, but my point is, that I must now live and implement this title that I have had the honor of receiving and use it only for the good of the community. A King serves the people, not the other way around.

Anthony: How long have you been doing Hip Hop activism and in what ways have you engaged in Hip Hop activism? Can you tell us some successful Hip Hop activist events you have organized and participated in and why they were success-ful in your opinion?

Reies: Throughout my twenties I was DJing heavily. For the most part, that is how I made a living, and I always knew there was a deeper meaning and purpose for my involvement in Hip Hop beyond the party or entertainment aspect of it. When my wisdom and experience increased, so did my realization of the power of Hip Hop as a whole, and how it can bring about real change and be a platform for justice. I threw myself into college and at the same time started to study Hip Hop history more; reading, listening, reading more, traveling, joining Save the Kids, Omega Zuluz (ZU), creating workshops that were unique and presenting them, learning from my local peers, elders and networking with other community orga-nizations. To put it simply, elevating my thinking and holding myself accountable to the best I could according to my evolving abilities. My conversion to the reli-gion of Islam helped shape this new way of thinking and how I viewed Hip Hop. Islam and Hip Hop have a very deep connection. Some overlook this aspect of the culture, but this is a long, detailed conversation which little will suffice here.

Hip Hop activism is really about teaching and learning. With Hip Hop in its fifth decade since its inception, it is our duty as activists to teach the history, as B-boys and B-girls, aerosol artists, DJ's, MC's, or simply Hip Hop heads and beyond. Teach with our heart and minds, and with relevant information that can reach the youth today to increase their potential in all that they do, in all aspects of their lives. The formula is there, we just have to have different flavors to reach a wide array of demographics. If you're a dancer such as B-boy J-Sun, you may use dance as your tool to teach. If you're a producer, you may use production skills to teach. A DJ, such as myself, uses the art of DJing. MCs like Toki Wright or Desdamona use the art of poetry, delivery, etc. Others, such as school teachers and college professors can use the elements and principles of Hip Hop as a learning tool for their students. White teachers are part of the problem in this country. Too many students of color are being taught by someone who doesn't look like them, share their experiences or identity and this is very problematic. Our entire U.S. educational system is problematic because ultimately it is taught through a European lens and reinforces the false ideology of white supremacy. Yes, you have heard this before, right? Of course you have and you will continue to hear about it until drastic measures are taken. More schools like CDF Freedom School are needed. Hip Hop education can teach reading, math, science and even Phys-Ed. Music as a whole can do this as well, even if a student is not into Hip Hop, it still can be used as a universal teaching mechanism. The Annual International Hip Hop Activism Conference put on by Save the Kids is a great example of Hip Hop learning. The 206 Zulu 15th Anniversary that took place in Seattle this past January is another great family friendly community event and it's free. Even Soundset, which is coordinated by RhymeSayers Entertainment, is a prime of example of Hip Hop culture and is one of the biggest Hip Hop festivals in the world right here in Minnesota. There are so many other excellent examples of Hip Hop focused learning and culture around the world as well.

Anthony: In what ways do you see Hip Hop activism growing and being needed both in society and within the realm of Hip Hop? What are some campaigns that Hip Hop activists are pushing and working on right now, and should be working on now or in the future?

Reies: I view every artist, Graff, B-boy and B-girl, DJ, MC, Hip Hop Professor or Teacher has a responsibility to the masses to teach, to create unity, empower our youth and create true equality, but at the same time not empower the status quo (i.e. white supremacy). Hip Hop is so engrained in our culture in the West that it should be taught in schools, community centers, homes and places of employment. Many forefathers of the culture have either passed away or are reaching their life's end; therefore, preserving this culture is so very crucial at this present time. It is mandatory for people like myself, and countless others, to take on this responsibility of teaching future generations. We must have accurate and viable sources in doing so. Like any other culture, religion, or civilization, lies have crept in and have been inserted by devious or ill-informed people. There will always be activism, there will always be Hip Hop, and putting the two together is just the next logical step. It is obvious and it is mandatory, in my opinion.

Hip Hop activism starts with self, knowledge of self, one's strengths and limitations; one's infinite potential must be harnessed and cultivated to become seasoned. I myself am still learning. I must re-read, re-listen, correct myself with any new, viable information that comes my way. I have to love the people in order to teach them, otherwise what's the point? I have to think the best of everyone I encounter no matter what color they are and build bridges. What do I mean by building bridges? It means I connect with others that I want to build the bridge with and we walk across it together. Do I see myself working hand in hand with Trump supporters? No, because ultimately they are my open enemy and an enemy of any person of color who has consciousness of who they are. The term "People of Color" to me means 'People of Color who are conscious of who they are, mind, body and soul' because there are so many so-called "POC" that are lost and will do anything to support white supremacy. Supporters of #45 are all around me. Every day, myself and others encounter people who support white supremacy whether they know it or not, openly or secretly. Hip Hop is a unifier, but the same white listener of Hip Hop will lean towards the status quo and the advancement of white supremacy. Sometimes they are not aware that this is occurring within themselves because the sheer fascination of Hip Hop blinds them. The so-called white listener must be informed of their guest position in a Black and Brown art form. I'm not saying that whites can't listen to Hip Hop, I am simply stating that it is not their invention or their place to appropriate it disrespectfully to the creators of the culture or co-opt it as in the case of Rock 'N Roll which, too, was the creation of Blacks. Whites have always had a fascination with Black music and art forms; it goes as far back as Muddy Waters and countless others. I believe Hip Hop can create its own political party, its own movement, and this movement's sole purpose would be for the empowerment of Black, Brown, indigenous, and the poor all around the world. There are already many Hip Hop activism circles and organizations around the world. There have been for a while, it's just that the mainstream media doesn't pay close attention to them and the media is the source of information for billions. One must dig deep and seek viable sources of underground information.

I believe firmly in Hip Hop being implanted, funded and respected in education. It is to some extent, but not to the point that it should be because not enough school councils, and administrators view it as viable. Even so-called people of color in these positions, they would rather switch the focus to "ethnic studies" which, on the whole I agree with, but why can't Hip Hop be a part of that mission and vision? The answer is it can be, it will be. Activists such as myself and countless others just have to "learn how to move in a room full of vultures" (Jay -Z, Izzo, H.O.V.A.).

Another way to implement Hip Hop education is by starting our own schools, our own community centers, our own programs that could be facilitated out of libraries, someone's basement or home, or an apartment community room, but it is not that simple. This takes a collective consciousness, effort, planning and so much more, not to mention funding. Organizations that provide grants are excited about funding a Hip Hop project, but funding an entire school is a different tale. One of my long-term goals before my inevitable death is to establish and open the doors to the first Minnesota Hip Hop Museum, dedicated to our rich and unique history of how we have experienced this culture. I will and I can, believe me. This dream must first be a dream, then a vision, then a mission, then the "work" must be put in. Nothing is handed to you, one must go get it, seize every moment and opportunity to achieve set goals and objectives. The scene here in Minnesota is all over the map, if you ask me. It has become over saturated with folks with little to no talent, yet we have our gems and jewels of the city, the artists that live, love and cherish their art form and it really shows when it is witnessed live. One can tell in a live act whether someone is genuine about their craft or not, at least that is the way it is for me.

My final piece of advice would be to be yourself, find your strengths and harness those strengths to be the best you can be at any given moment. One must harness areas of growth as well, to understand what you are not actually capable of and realize that is okay. Embrace these perceived fears and transform them into power, create a coping mechanism that is strong for the advancement of your own soul. Many of us have experienced trauma in some form or fashion; how strong is our individual and collective resilience to said trauma and what is our final outcome and destination? Together we can create a power greater than anyone in political office or corporate position. We can create a world of true equality, justice and harmony. One of my heroes Chuck D once said, *"Knowledge, wisdom and understanding don't come out of a microwave. You have to keep moving forward because the evil doesn't sleep."* If evil never sleeps then neither can we. Life moves very quickly. The key is making every moment count with meaning and purpose. Now that I am "over the hill" I know my purpose. In my twenties I didn't exactly know what it was. People develop in different ways and we have to accept folks where they are in life. Hip Hop is life, just like water is, just like one's smiles and cries, like one's waking and sleeping hours. All praise is due to Allah (SWT) and if you are reading this and have felt what I have written, know that I Love You and that I am here, so if you see me, hug me. Zulu King Reies.

CHAPTER FIVE

Interview with Katrina Benally

CHANDRA WARD

Chandra: How did I get started with my music?

Katrina: I have always been influenced by music. I remember when I got my first portable cassette tape player for Christmas, when I was young. It was freedom compared to listening to tapes on my parent's huge system in the living-room. I could listen to music wherever I went, and my family traveled a lot. My parents are Native American jewelers and they used to vend at jewelry shows across the country. I also have to give my parents credit for showing me the music that would later influence my sounds. They showed me artists like Journey, Bob Marley, Ozzy Osbourne, and the list goes on. I had always been interested in Hip Hop and rap music but I had to kind of seek that out on my own. I only knew songs that I liked, not even artists or their albums, and sometimes I didn't even know the name of the song, but when it came on the radio or at the skating rink I used to hang out at, I would start jamming. After that, rap and Hip Hop became my top two favorite genres with rock. And I say top two because one could be number one one day and the other could be number one the next day. But through that, I learned about artists like Notorius B.I.G., Bone Thugs-N-Harmony, Ol' Dirty Bastard, Outkast, Puff Daddy, Eminem, and that list can go on as well.

Then in high school is when I got into bands like Red Hot Chili Peppers, Incubus, and a bunch of random indie rock my friend, Erin, used to put on these mix CDs for me. I would hear bands like Weezer, Death Cab for Cutie, and

Interpol. So now, I'm looking around and people are playing guitar. I think it's the coolest thing since I was around 4 or 5. I thought it would be the most amazing thing to be a rock star. I'm pretty sure my parents have a picture of me rocking out on a toy guitar and standing on top of a little table like it was my stage. I also asked my parents to buy me plenty of toy guitars when I was young.

So anyway, I'm 14, I found out about "tabs" when it comes to learning how to play guitar and I'm getting excited because I once took a lesson and it was so boring. I did not have the patience to learn notes. Now, I've learned that you don't need to know notes, there's tabs! Tabulature. So, I started learning how to play Incubus, Blink 182, Red Hot Chili Peppers, and Pantera guitar intros. I'm realizing now that I've always taught myself when it came to learning instruments. I learned to play "My Heart Will Go On" by Celine Dion on the keyboard when I was 9 or 10. I also learned Savage Garden's "Truly, Madly, Deeply." The keyboard my parents gave me came with some pictures that showed you which keys to press after I labeled them with notes. I didn't even realize I was playing notes now that I'm talking about this. At the time, in my mind set, I was also very much into drawing, so I was very visual, but I just saw "label this key 'A', this key 'B' and then press this key 'A' and this key," and so forth and then, all of sudden, I was playing the song. After more practice, I was able to play without my book. I stopped playing the keyboard around the same time. I'm not sure why kids get bored quickly.

Now, back to playing guitar. I started playing guitar at 14 and that continued through high school. I went to the University of Arizona after I graduated. While living in Tucson, Arizona, I learned about the song "Chronic" and those new friends showed me crazy amounts of rap and Hip Hop. They even showed me songs that had been "chopped and screwed," which is some of the coolest music I have ever heard. Unfortunately, some things happened and I had to move back home and I felt like such a loser. But I signed up for the Branch College in Gallup, New Mexico and did a year of school there as well. Since I was back at home, I had this poster on the wall in my room that showed you where to put your fingers to learn chords on the guitar. After doing homework, I would just sit and start learning these chords. Well, the ones I liked the most anyway. And then I go through a break-up and I started to think I had nothing to lose anymore. I don't care if I embarrass myself, so I decide "I'm going to fucking write a song. I'm going to sing." I told myself that and then I wrote my first indie rock acoustic song. And the four that followed are some of the most depressing songs I ever wrote, but hey music is for that. A place to put your sadness. Your happiness. Your madness. Your everything's, if that makes sense. I know it's not grammatically correct but yeah, your everything's. You can put whatever you want into a song.

Next, I can't stop thinking about rapping. I had always written poetry but there had never been a Navajo Girl Rapper or a Native Female rapper of any sort that I had heard of. I knew that if I did this, I could be talked down or I would get the feeling that no one believed I could be a rapper. And that's exactly what happened. But I just didn't stop making rap music. I taught myself how to make beats and record my vocals with a USB mic. My first official rap single was called, "If You Can Do It, I Can Do It." And at the time I was hearing mainly Drake and Kid Cudi on the radio, but then I heard Kesha and I was just thrown off. No offense against Kesha but she really made me think "Ok, if this chick can do this then I can too." I also thought that if I tried and failed, I would just be right where I was again, at home in my room. Good thing I kept going, too, because now I'm answering questions to be featured in a book. This book. Which is something I never even considered would take place.

Chandra: May I ask how you identify in terms of your gender and sexuality?

Katrina: I identify as a female lesbian but I don't mind the they/him pronouns. I've run into some people that have called me sir and I don't know, it just felt silly to correct them. Because what if it was out of respect? What if they thought I was maybe transitioning? And they were trying to be cool? Or were they really being rude and making fun of me as a tomboy? And I'm just clueless? Who knows. I always smile, though, and tell them to have a good day. I don't always get a "good day" back but it's all alright. I have literally reached a point in my life where issues like that are unworthy of my time. And at the end of the day, I know that I like to dress 'like a boy," so why should I feel bothered if someone addresses me like a boy. The same concept applies for the "they" pronoun. I'm also not as "filled out" as most girls in the boobs and ass areas, so I'm sure people wonder if I'm trans or not. I also wonder if I should consider some of my guy friends trans or not because their boobs are much bigger than I ever seen on any woman sometimes. That includes big dudes and body builders. They get their pecks so big. Like seriously big. Like get a bra, I have to wear one and mine are not even close to being that big! And I know some douche is going to read this and say something like "you don't have to wear a bra" for his benefit. Also, at this time, as I write this, sexual assault cases are coming up like crazy and that's without women being topless in public like dudes. Am I getting off topic? My bad. Anyway, I used to wear my hair down a lot, so it was easy to tell then, but lately for the past four to five years, I've been rocking my braids pretty hard. I think most people that know me now are surprised to see me with my hair down. And, at this time in my life, it definitely makes me feel blessed to be in situations where I can see things through other human eyes as much as I can. Perspectives are underrated in society; I think we could learn a lot from them. I'll admit, I didn't realize some things I needed to work on until I heard certain people's perspectives. But in "my" perfect world, I would like to identify as Human from Planet Earth or a Planet Earthling.

Chandra: How does your identity and background inform your music and your activism? Can you give some examples?

Katrina: I like to think my identity is my music. And that includes everything, from my acoustic sad rock, to a real dope lo-fi beat, singing to a chill Hip Hop production, and to my funky fast raps on a house-style beat. I love to express myself in many ways with music. I hate to put limits on myself or the things that I do. There is so much music out there, the way I see it, the more music, the better. If an artist can do well in many genres, that's pretty amazing. I want to live my life to at least "try' and be that type of artist. There are people out here in the world acting, making music, and doing comedy. That's super cool to me. I love multi-tasking. Therefore, my music is multi-genre, to me. I love expressing myself vocally through rapping more than singing. But I love singing when its improvisational, unplanned, and I can just be spontaneous (e.g., do hum or do "la's"). I do a lot of that with the band, Pray for Brain.

In my activism, the same applies. I am just myself. And a huge part of that, at the time that I write this, is still learning activism. Activism is a chess game, but so is life. You have and you need people to be at different levels working together, not just physically, but even just thoughtfully or spiritually, and I am not talking about religion. It's just heart. Maybe it's soul too. I feel we as people do not acknowledge our souls as much as we should. I also believe that activism is something you should practice daily, or at least try to. I am definitely not perfect at that, not even close, and it depends on who you talk to as well. Different people in activism are still thinking differently from the person next to them, but they're still working towards the same goal. So, those two people could have different opinions about my activism. One might really like it and the other one could say I haven't done shit.

With that being said, I believe I am an activist in my music, with what I write in my lyrics. I believe I am an activist when I do youth workshops for the underprivileged kids on reservations. I believe I am an activist when I am on stage with my partner, Letsjusb, as two women, two lesbian women, might I add, and we are usually the only two women in almost every Hip Hop lineup, everywhere we go. And we usually kill it, I like to think anyway. And that alone is threatening to the heteropatriarchy that controls the rap game. No backup vocals when we hit the stage, trust that. Moving on, I also think I am an activist when I'm simply sharing knowledge on Facebook, because I'm friends with the local male-dominated Hip Hop scene in my state, and some surrounding states, and I'm friends with a lot of Native women and guys of all ages from all over the nation. Of course, I have other friends that just make up the mix but when I post things that usually cause a riot online, it's usually stuff that is so simple. Like the time I upset some legendary MC for just wanting to be called my name, my first name, and not dear.

He got so hurt about that and ultimately destroyed our friendship because he just got creepy about it. But he was hurt at the same time. It blows my mind how easily these guys get hurt over something that has to do with how I identify and not with how they identify. Their logic is so toxic. But the underlying message of that post was to let women know that they deserve to be called their name and ultimately, they deserve respect from the very first greeting. No pet names. And that ultimately was my little move towards bringing down patriarchy a little bit. Subliminal messaging and move making, unfortunately, but the society learns that way. I'm ready to pay for a billboard to advertise for peace and love real soon because society learns with ads so quickly. It's sad. So, I have to switch up how I'm going to deliver the message.

So, no, I am not on the front lines at Standing Rock or anywhere else, but like I said, this is chess not checkers. Those people in the frontlines are the strongest people I know. The most courageous. I really want to salute them every time I meet someone who went to the frontlines. Because I've been to jail, and it's terrible. And they are always willing to risk that. I just can't. That's not my position on the chess board; my position requires me to stay out of jail because of all the other work I am doing. I believe that for other people on the frontlines. I really hope that they took that passion from the frontlines and brought it back to their people and then I hope they take it around the world as far as they can, in whatever it is they do. We need more successful Natives in the world than ones that go to jail and get stuck in the system. But I am thankful for those people; if they weren't on the frontlines at Standing Rock, I probably wouldn't be writing this interview for this book.

Chandra: Hip Hop is male dominated do you feel like as a woman you have to "do" Hip Hop a certain way to gain respect?

Katrina: This is a tough one to answer because when I started making music, I knew I would have to get into the mindset and accept that a lot of people might not like my music. Or maybe the whole world because, yes, I am a woman, a Native lesbian trying to rap. "Who would support that?! … No one", I thought. My family already wasn't giving me the reactions I wish I would have received and my little sister was listening to Tech Nine, like a hardcore fan. Whenever I played music for her, she wasn't impressed. I was never hurt about it or anything, like I thought I was as good as Tech. I just took it as constructive criticism that I need to get better, of course. Because of this "mindset" I was already in, I never worried about "gaining respect." Especially from males. I acted like there was no respect to gain. Like it wasn't a thing that I would let affect how I put out my music. The world is filled with so many different opinions, likes and dislikes, that I knew that a small part of the world would like the kind of music I was going to do. Little did I know, it was going to be the Hip Hop scene.

Now, the Hip Hop scene in Albuquerque (ABQ), New Mexico is male dominated like any other Hip Hop scene but ABQ doesn't mess around when it comes to pure Hip Hop and how it is performed. They give props when it's due, for sure. For example, no one respects an MC that raps over their vocals during public performances. You just can't call yourself an MC and no one will call you an MC for doing that. Are there rappers getting mainstream views and getting discovered? Yes, but they're rapping over vocals. I roll with the people that respect the work ethic it takes to nail your flows on stage while jumping around and keeping things hype. It's a lot of adrenaline and cardio. People rapping over vocals need that background help because they do get tired but not from rapping and exercising their vocals. No, they get tired most likely from head-banging on stage too hard. Now, some people will debate about what is the pure Hip Hop scene in the ABQ music scene. I believe it is the ones that get booked and are booking old school greats like members from Wu-Tang and their affiliates. I mean does it get any more Hip Hop than that?

I also have to be careful now that I am more aware of how many dudes and great MC's engaged in sexual assault, or any form of human-hating, either recently or over the years. If I found out you're doing any of that, I really don't care about getting that person's respect. Like Eminem is one of my favorite rappers and Immortal Technique's "Dance with the Devil" is one the of the greatest songs I ever heard, but they have both rapped about assaulting women, whether it was true or untrue. Words are so powerful coming from people like that, so you have to worry about its influence. However, a part of me is forgiving, because I can't deny their artistry and the experience it stemmed from, or the fact that art is meant for things like this. I hope they both wrote their evil lyrics and then never committed actions like that again, or I hope it helped heal the anger or depression they were probably experiencing. Back to the question of gaining respect, I'm sure I would have to do music a certain way to gain respect from certain people but for the most part, I don't care enough to impress anyone. I don't think about that or worry about gaining respect like that. I give respect to you until you give me a reason to take it away and vice versa. Sometimes, it takes time to see those reasons, and other times, it can take a few minutes of just being in someone's presence. After writing this, I realize now, that Hip Hop respects a lot of people that just don't care about people's respect when it comes to their music.

Chandra: How do people respond/receive you as an indigenous woman in this medium/genre of music—in doing hip-hop? Has that been more or less challenging than your sexual identity in this genre or music?

Katrina: I can't really speak for people and how they respond to me unless they tell me themselves and I haven't been told too many comments about this specific question. But I can offer my opinion on how I think people respond to me and I think the only people responding to me as an "indigenous woman" in Hip Hop are other indigenous peoples because they know where we come from. They know there are no Native female rappers, so, I feel like I was one of the firsts to make it somewhere to even make people begin to think about it—a Diné Woman rapper/MC. Other Hip Hop heads, musicians, and co-artists don't even worry about things like that. They worry about whether you got the skills or not and that's it. They also don't care that I'm a lesbian. If anything, I think the real artists know that we need more artists being themselves to the fullest with no limits, no labels, or any restraints. But there are people that have been a part of the Hip Hop world forever, it seems, and they still carry themselves like they don't accept gay or trans people or even people that want water over oil. These days are crazy. Some of those people maybe avoid booking me for shows or whatever. I would never know if they did or not though, but I'm sure it might have happened. Either way, I'm connecting with positive people and that's all I need or want. I'm lucky that the only thing that is challenging in all of this, for me, is managing my career or lack thereof. But I think that's a good problem to have, sounds like I need a real manager soon.

Chandra: Can you tell me about the social justice work you do both in and outside of your community? How is this connected to your music if at all?

Katrina: You know, I used to think there were only a few ways "to do social justice work." I thought it was going to Standing Rock or other peaceful protests, or I thought it was being a social justice lawyer or just a regular judge in court. And then the Hip Hop duo I'm in got asked to perform at a fundraiser show in Winslow, Arizona to bring awareness to police brutality and essentially racism in border towns. A border town is a "town" usually near the New Mexico and Arizona state-line and its majority population is Indigenous. So, the fundraiser was for a funeral and legal fees for the family of Loreal Tsinigini. That was one of the top three shows in my experience so far, that I would say changed my life or really provided a perspective that I was missing or had not learned about yet, if that makes sense. There's a real power in music and you can use it to help influence. Obviously, major companies use artists all the time to make their new company "look cool," but this event wasn't like that. It was for a much deeper reason, a much deeper cause, and it would never get as much exposure as it deserves. At that event for Loreal, we met her family including Loreal's daughter and they saw us perform. I cried when we met Loreal's daughter. You feel like you want to do something for her to help heal the pain but what can you do? We rapped for 20 minutes and we hope that was inspiring more than influencing. We didn't even know this family but somehow, we all felt connected. We all felt wronged.

Loreal's aunties cried and we cried with them. Loreal would've been 28, I believe, if she were still alive and I'm her same age. If that were me that day in Winslow, face to face to with that same cop, I can't help but wonder if I would have met the same outcome. Empathy can be more personal than we think sometimes. I think that's why it's something society tries to avoid doing. It is literally a lot, sometimes too much to take on because who needs more stress these days, right? I'm going off on another note but it still relates. I'm not sure how performing for a cause is a form of social justice work but things like this need to be talked about and they need more support from everyone. The more we talk about it, the more people will show concern for these problems and not things like who's winning the Super Bowl. We have to make "social justice" cool, somehow. That's why I do shows that work towards things like that, as well, like fundraisers for legal fees for protesters being arrested on the frontlines.

Another form of social justice work I do is just speaking on things, whether it's on social media or with random, one-on-one conversations I find myself in. My day job, right now, is working at a retail shop in an area where there are a lot of tourists, and I mean a lot. I talk to a lot of people, I've met a lot of cool people through that job. A cool story is that I once spoke with a descendant from Queen Isabel, a nephew, all the way and directly from Spain. Remember Queen Isabel gave money to Columbus to sail to the Americas back in the day. So, I was kind of in shock like "Wow, this could make history if it were a different Native having this conversation right now." Or if it happened somewhere else and not in this retail shop next to a cash register. This guy was not afraid to speak about how "fighting terrorism since 1492" is a false statement. So, we talked about it. We ended the conversation not agreeing on anything but we shook hands. We spoke on the whole matter of Columbus coming here to Turtle Island. We weren't afraid to talk about the genocide and forced religion and how that played into the creation of an economy. It was an intense conversation but it was so civil. Our manners were on point, if I say so myself. But actions and reactions like that in public, I believe count for more than anything when it comes to "social justice work." I think a lot of people feel like they're not important enough to speak up or say things that speak on change or sound different from the "norm." Or it's never the "right time" or "let's not get political.' Most political viewpoints will tell you whether or not a person values life over certain things or not and that can teach you a lot about a person too. And I'll say this, all the greatest people I have met or know want more people to live than die. It's cool to think that, ok? Just letting you readers know because advertisements, reality tv shows, and video games will try to convince you otherwise. Let people know when they're being mean or hurting people. We always have more than enough people dying as it is; the pointless and undeserving deaths really need to come to an end.

Moving on to other forms of "social justice" work I believe I do is just inspiring the youth. Mainly to help steer them away from getting into situations that might get them arrested or jailed. It's terrible once you're in the system, and I can speak from experience. Especially if you're Native. Try your absolute hardest to stay out that place and just put more work into becoming successful. That's the only way I see our people getting the respect we deserve. We're smart, we're talented, and we are survivors. So, adapt to some cool stuff, have some fun, and become a star. We need as many of you as possible to at least try. A lot of Indigenous peoples are getting some nice recognition for their talents. We're all a bunch of Rezzies (i.e., Native Americans from reservations) and we are all still proud of that too. And that's why I am a part of a group of people, an art collective/Hip Hop crew that was started by Bishop Undurdog that hosts free art workshops for the youth on Indigenous reservations, but all youth are always welcome. The group is proud of its Indigenous roots and of their existence as modern artists. So we feel like the youth need to see people like that, especially people that look like them doing things like rapping and helping their communities. Unfortunately, the reservation is also known to be heavy with gang activity. Whether you want to believe it or not, things are intense on the reservation because the cops are like 20–40 minutes, sometimes an hour away, before they can reach a scene in time to actually do something about it. So, we believe the arts and the muscle memory they gain from participating in these workshops will keep them from living a gang life or at least help them discover the artist that is already in them and maybe that will lead them to a positive life. Nothing is for sure but we believe we have to try. Growing up as a Native American, it's all about insecurities. We have been taught to hate everything about ourselves and that started when they cut the braids off our ancestors. That is another part of these workshops, when we bring in the Hip Hop and speakers. The kids see the artists go from helping them with the workshops, to the stage to rock the microphone, and they notice they're not that bad, either. But they also notice that they are Native and we hope they see themselves in what we do and maybe with that, some hope will be restored. We want to make it a "cool" thing to acknowledge your Indigenous roots. We always tell them if you work hard enough you can make money doing something like screen-printing or wood-burning. Which is why we do so many workshops at a time. And they're always free to participate. We provide everything and it's funded by us. We are not rich but we give back to our community a lot quicker than a lot of other "rich" rappers. Yeah, they probably spoiled their families but they could really repair and heal some communities with a small portion of the cash they're probably making. The artist, Drake, is still doing just fine after giving away almost a million dollars in that God's Plan video and there are people out there that are a lot wealthier than him.

Chandra: What are you working on right now?

Katrina: A lot. I have a lot of new material and projects on the way. I don't know what to say because I don't know when this chapter will see the light of day. It'll be a different "right now" and I am always working on music and four other different creative things depending on the day. So, look up "k.benally" and "kbenallyletsjusb" on social media to keep up with me, thanks.

Chandra: Is there anything you would like to add that perhaps you want people to know about you?

Katrina: Yeah, I'm not perfect

CHAPTER SIX

Interview with Selinda Guerrero

AHMAD WASHINGTON

Ahmad: How long have you been involved in activism and in what issues?

Selinda: I think maybe I was born an activist … I remember always caring about justice and fairness even when I didn't know what it was called. A true turning point for me was when I became a mother just after my 16th birthday. At the time I was still hustling as my income. I was an 8th grade pushout of Washington Middle School and had been in the streets since 13. This particular night, the smokers kept waking my baby up. I was getting frustrated as a new mother and in the morning, I told my son's dad that we had to stop selling dope. He thought I was crazy but I just suddenly realized my son could not have our same destiny, he deserved better. I left his dad and moved with my mom and signed up for every program I could find. I started meeting all these dope non-profits, organizers and activists. I remember thinking "why didn't we know they were here?" By age 17, I was all in, creating videos to apply for grant funding for our programs, facilitating our groups and marching on the state legislature to try to stop Clinton's Welfare Reform Act. I have never stopped being involved in the movement since.

I wanted to understand and speak to what my community was experiencing. I needed to find my voice. I needed to tell the truth about my experience and the experience of my people.

Currently, most of my work has been in prison abolition, the school to prison pipeline, and issues concerning poverty and the struggle. I think prison has always existed in my life. I remember being very young, maybe 3 or 4 years old, and my mom would take me with her to visit family in the north, Santa Fe Main Prison. This was right around the time of the notorious Santa Fe Prison riots. I grew up in an environment where police violence, criminalization, and incarceration were a normal part of our neighborhoods.

I think I was 12 or 13 years old the first time the police gang unit profiled me. They used to stop us on the street and take our pictures then ask us where we were from. I learned early, we do not talk to the police. It was always apparent they were not for us.

I experienced many traumas in my childhood from sexual abuse, violence, poverty, but the experiences that had the greatest impact were the issues around death. Several times I was supposed to be killed, but wasn't. So many people I knew were dying, that I had a ritual for every funeral I went to as a teen; I would take a single red rose to the mother. I always hoped that when I died someone would do that for my mom, that they would show her love and help her understand it was not her fault. I think I was so reckless because I believed I would not live very long.

I talk about that now when I am discussing Juvenile Justice issues. When young people have nothing to live for, we are capable of anything. I firmly believe reconciling with that fact is essential in school to prison pipeline issues. We must address and support young people in the struggle who are living in trauma. It is painful and young people struggle to understand we can still survive; an early death is not inevitable. If you would have asked the 15-year-old me if I would be alive today—I'd say you're crazy, hell no.

For some reason I never got hooked on dope, went to prison, or died. That was the fate of nearly everyone from that part of my life. I believe I survived for a reason and that reason is to be a truth teller and change maker for my people. I understand now that the socioeconomic issues that brought me so much trauma were not my fault and is not the fault of my people. It was intentional institutions of oppression that have been in place since the founding of this country that is rooted in slavery and genocide.

Ahmad: What elements of Hip Hop have you been involved with and influenced by?

Selinda: For me, Tupac was always my prophet. He spoke for us when we didn't have a voice. He advocated for our well-being and told the rest of the world how we were living. Tupac said the things we didn't know how to articulate and gave us the knowledge we weren't getting in school. His lyrics are as relevant today as they ever have been. I was going to name some out but there are too many that are still really, really real for us.

Nas was another artist that deeply influenced me. He kicked knowledge as a scholarly lyricist. Always telling us to do better, telling the truth about our history, and gave imagination for what could be if we were truly liberated. "If I Ruled the World" makes you imagine what could really be possible if we had the power to create the world we wish we had. What could it be like if we could free all who are enslaved in the prisons, feed all the hungry and, more importantly, just feel joy and happiness?

I remember when Ice Cube's "Lynch Mobb" came out, we went to the music store to get it. I think we played it back to back for a week straight. Or Dr. Dre's "Chronic" was another one you could play all the way through. West coast Hip Hop was deep for us because it spoke to what we experienced in our neighborhoods not being able to leave our hood without a gun and some homies. You were always in danger if you got caught outside your neighborhood alone. Gangs were so prevalent in my city growing up that for survival we had to be creative with ways to navigate the city without having to claim a hood. I created the "Sesame Street" gang as a means of survival. We took characters from PBS' Sesame Street and named ourselves; I was Elmo. We would clown folks who were claiming hoods and the police when they tried to profile us. They would ask what are you claiming, we would respond "Sesame Street." This actually made it into the gang unit book.

Hip Hop was never just music for me; it was my life. My older cousins turned me on to Hip Hop. I cannot remember how old I was but probably preschool or kindergarten when I would carry the stereo for my cousin to the basketball courts. I had to work to kick it with the older kids. I remember "Rappers Delight"—I couldn't believe what I was hearing … Then came UTFO, "Sally that Girl," the "Show, Doug E. Fresh," "Egyptian Lover," and everyone was break-dancers and busting flows back then. We did not leave home without our stereo.

Then the clothes came, and you had to get parachute pants with the zippers, net half shirt. We were poor but somehow, we came up on some fashion. I was fortunate to have older cousins that were always dressed in the newest styles so hand-me-downs got me through. We are West Coast in my city so also "chucks" and "dickies" dominated our swag. The jewelry and gear were part of showing we were making it; we are not just surviving, we have value. Having the coolest rims, systems, jewelry, and fresh clothes was our way of reinforcing our existence. When the world treats you like you have no value, what better way to challenge that narrative than to show out.

Slick Rick was another that spoke to me from the very beginning. I remember I got his bootleg cassette tape at the flea market and it read "blank turn over" on both sides. I thought "Children's Story" was the best song ever and "A Teenage Love" ran deep even when we didn't know anything about love. Hip Hop showed me what love should be and how much it can hurt when it goes bad. I cried to LL Cool J's "I Need Love" during my first heartbreak. I can recite every word of that song and felt it deep in my soul. Even today, crazy love songs like Kevin Gates' "We Supposed to be in Love" have been part of my breakups. Hip Hop has been there when I fell in love, during great relationships, and during crucial breakups. I learned how to love through Hip Hop. I always said if I were to ever get married my wedding song is going to be "You're All I Need to Get Bby" by Method Man and Mary J. Blige; it is the best love song.

NWA was a turning point for me. You see we always experienced police violence but when "F**k the Police" came out, it felt like liberation; it was empowerment in a way I hadn't felt before. To play that song all the way turned up when the police rolled through was power! I did not fully understand law enforcements' role in this country but I knew they were never for us. From a very young age, I naturally feared them; thinking back, I think it came from my community. There were always things spoken and unspoken that let me know we should never trust them. Then as I spent more time in the streets and they began to see me and my friends as a threat, I really felt the force of what police violence can be. In my city, police had a "gang unit" that used to stop us walking in our neighborhoods all the time, our city's version of stop and frisk. The "gang unit" used to stop us and take our pictures, question, and search us. They had such a presence when it was time to harass us but when someone shot up our house or died in my neighborhood, they did not even show up. I remember when a guy I knew from another neighborhood came banging in my neighborhood and the homies shot and killed him. His body stayed on the street for almost 24 hours before the police came to pick his body up. I cannot even count how many instances of police violence I've witnessed or heard about from my community, as well as all who have been murdered by them.

Female artists were the dopest. When Queen Latifah came out with "U.N.I.T.Y." we were all running around talking about "Who you callin a b***h?" Or when Roxanne came back at UTFO. Awe, the best was Miss Thang coming back at Orange Juice Jones with "Thunder and Lighting!" As a young female, it was empowering to know I could stand up to anyone if my words were tight. I did not know the word "misogyny" or "patriarchy" as a young person but I knew being female I was always treated as less valuable or only viewed as a sexual object. I was a tomboy growing up and always hung with the boys playing street football, basketball, and acting up in the streets. Everything changed when puberty hit. I was immediately physically developed and the boys, my friends, never saw me the same. Street football turned into attempts to feel me up and a whole lot of fighting. I cannot count how many boys I fought during that time in my life because I was fighting for the only existence and acceptance I knew. It was not fair that I was suddenly being seen differently; my body changed but who I was inside hadn't. I needed the strength and power that female artists provided; they expressed my same struggle.

Recently, I was on a Hip Hop internet radio show "Shut Up and Talk" discussing the movement and LB Johnson said "Every time Selinda comes through it sounds like she dropin bars"—I think I learned young to just spit it, don't give them space to come back, just drop the knowledge. So definitely, the lyricist, emceeing, is the element that resonates. I did not have the talent of being a b-girl, tagger, or djing but everyone always told me my mouth is cold and do not mess with it because I will hurt your feelings. I never much wrote my own rhymes but have always spoke with the rhythm of a beat.

Ahmad: How do you relate Hip Hop to your activism and can you give us ways to do it and examples?

Selinda: Our Hip Hop artists today are still speaking for us. At a rally just last week against the NRA and Police Violence, we had the "FDT" (F**k Donald Trump) song by YG on the loud speaker. Many artists today are still saying the things many in my community are fighting to say. Artists like Kendrick Lamar and J-Cole are still speaking truth to power about our ghettos and the prison industrial complex.

In this political climate songs like "F**k Donald Trump" are important to our movements. It is the same fight we have always been in against racism and capitalism. With the attack on our communities being ramped up, this song has become today's "F**k the Police."

Every event I put on has spoken word poetry, Hip Hop, and graffiti art banners. Especially the works in progress, we have so much talent in our communities they need to be platformed the most. Hip Hop helps our people find their voice and power; it is who we are, it is in our soul and in every part of our lives. So, an open mic and cypher are critical parts to our organizing structure. We want to ensure all our people have access to a platform and mic to be heard. Our people are screaming out to be heard and their words are critically important because as Glenn Martin emphasizes "those closest to the problem have the best solutions." I believe we can solve our own problems if we just empower each other to speak out in safe spaces where expression and empowerment can happen.

Every event I have ever organized had a mix of spoken word poetry and Hip Hop. It is literally how I organize. Hip Hop is how I found my voice, so I must pay homage anytime I am organizing for power.

Ahmad: Why is engaging in Hip Hop important when addressing prison abolition and youth justice?

Selinda: Hip Hop is the voice from the soul of the people. I think about the Bennie Segal song "What Ya Life Like"—I organize with folks behind the walls, and

Casino from Angola prison during the prison strike said that song was helping him maintain his sanity. Or the song by Z-Ro "Tired" that cuts deep. It is not about engagement you see; it is who we are.

With our young people, it is the talent our people know and are connected to, whether that's learning how to break dance from their big homie or flow while standing on the block. It is a culture we are deeply connected to; it is now our history; it is part of our movement; it is who we are.

Ahmad: What are key elements of promote and participating in Hip Hop activism?

Selinda: I do not like appropriation ... I think of what Naughty by Nature said "If you ain't never been to the ghetto, don't ever come to the ghetto, cause you wouldn't understand the ghetto ..." I think many are intrigued by Hip Hop but don't actually understand how deep it is; that it is in our souls and peculates from our ancestry of Blues, Jazz and Gospel.

We must honor and pay homage to Hip Hop—including all the elements in their true form are a part of that honoring. Staying authentic when we are organizing is key. We use our own platforms to promote. For example, flyers are still important even in this time of social media; radio is still important and we have access to several Hip Hop internet radio shows.

When organizing, I'm always thinking about how to use Hip Hop at our events and actions to help our community heal. Several songs were made in the name of Jaquise Lewis, our city's Trayvon Martin. Songs made for people murdered or harmed in our community and by people in our own communities is part of that healing. Public mourning and acts of civil disobedience are important in helping our community heal. At other times during events, we can use elements of Hip Hop to celebrate and build community through B-boying, cyphers, and beat boxing. I think one of the most powerful elements is graffiti art; the expression that is translated is pure brilliance. I have watched our people pour their souls into pieces created for our actions.

I think activism and organizing are arts all in themselves so just like any art, be authentic to who you are. If you were born in Hip Hop, like me, you must organize Hip Hop in all of its raw, graphic, and beautiful truthfulness.

Ahmad: When do you think you or others should not or cannot engage in Hip Hop activism?

Selinda: I cannot think of activism and organizing without Hip Hop. I have done actions where it was obvious that everyone could not relate but I think it is authentic to who we are so I would not change the way I organize. My community organizing is about the people, those impacted, those closest to the problem and, for the most part, they are Hip Hop. But, as I stated, if Hip Hop is not who you are and it is not in your soul, then perhaps Hip Hop activism will not speak to you.

But, regardless, it is an art that can be admired and respected by all. We see it globally. In the book by human rights activist Ishmael Beah, he discusses how Hip Hop saved his life during the civil wars in Sierra Leone. He also discussed how influential it was for his people. I also do work with Palestinian Liberation, and my Arab folks have shared their hip- hop videos with me. It is inspiring to see Hip Hop in other languages, accents and baselines liberating people around the world. So, I think Hip Hop activism has so much soul that it can resonate with anyone anywhere.

I think the very interest in this piece we are working on shows the power of Hip Hop activism. We know universities across the country study Hip Hop culture. Harvard has recently introduced a series where students dissect Hip Hop for a more thorough understanding and are invoking Hip Hop artists into their music library. I think we should be cautious, though. We must not allow Hip Hop to be colonized like so many of our other arts. It is a fine line between honor and assimilation. I caution those who do not have Hip Hop in their souls to admire and honor but not to destroy as colonialism has done to so much of our culture.

I feel protective of Hip Hop, like it is my elder and child. It is and will continue to evolve but it is important that it happens with authenticity. Will there one day be some version of "smooth jazz" by Kenny G in the Hip Hop world? Perhaps, it has already happened. Either way, me and my community will continue to love, mourn, and organize with Hip Hop. Most of all, we will continue to pay homage and work to preserve it for what it is: our culture, voice, soul and whole selves.

Ahmad: With the work you do with Save the Kids, can you tell us in details some events that were rooted in Hip Hop activism more than others that you have organized around?

Selinda: Save the Kids work is always rooted in Hip Hop. Every event or action has always included a Hip Hop vibe. It's hard to say that it was more than others since this is how I organize. Obviously, I have assisted others with actions where I spoke or supported that did not include Hip Hop but if I am the organizer, it will include Hip Hop and spoken word.

For Malcom X Day this year, we organized with our young people who were super ambitious. They presented a workshop by formerly homeless youth, then a discussion panel, and a civil disobedience action that ended with a Hip Hop show. Hip Hop is how we celebrate also. Even our chants during civil disobedience actions are in rhymes and always have been. I believe these elements have always been part of our organizing structure even before it was called Hip Hop.

Our young people made flyers to hand out at their schools with graffiti art. We provided space at the event where people could make their own posters using spray paint for a civil disobedience action. Our focus was on program kids, young people impacted by incarceration, houseless, and CYFD; Children Youth and Families in New Mexico otherwise known as Child Protective Services. These are our young people who need safe spaces to be their whole selves. Hip Hop environment provides that space whether standing in the street with a sign they created in civil disobedience or taking the mic and spitting a rhyme or spoken word poetry. This environment is healing but more importantly empowering where we can challenge each other to build community and solve problems.

I organize with our people behind the walls across the country. From California to South Carolina, Hip Hop is used through podcasts and workshops for our people to express and heal. I work with Decarcerate Louisiana and Free Alabama movements with graffiti art, poetry and Hip Hop to advance their movements.

Ahmad: If you were to speak to the larger Hip Hop community, what would you say and what do you see as wrong with Hip Hop now?

Selinda: Well, it's the Common song "I Used to Love Her" especially when he says "Hip Hop was underground, original, pure and untampered ..." Capitalism has done what it does to everything else; it destroys and corrupts. We have labels today controlling the voice of the people. We have to rely on the underground or artists who speak out despite being outcasted. The mainstream music today does not feel original, pure or untampered with; rather it feels commercialized and capitalist. I feel like it is giving a message of division and splinters our people instead of uniting them in the struggle. I am so grateful to Killa Mike, Meek Mill, J. Cole, Nipsy Hustle, and Kendrick Lamar for holding us down in today's music. We still have so much more work ahead of us before our people are liberated but I feel Hip Hop will continue to be part of the soul of our movement.

CHAPTER SEVEN

Interview with Antonio Quintana

AHMAD WASHINGTON

Ahmad: Tell me about your earliest recollections of Hip Hop culture and how you became connected to the culture?

Antonio: My earliest recollections of Hip Hop go back to 1993, when I was ten years old. I remember my older cousins were listening to the new albums that came out at that time—The Chronic, Black Sunday, etc. I was drawn to all the Hip Hop music that I heard but the album that really struck me was *Enter the Wu-Tang (36 Chambers)*. I quickly got hooked on listening to all the Hip Hop music I could get my hands on.

I became connected to the culture because I found exactly what I was looking for in Hip Hop. To be specific, at the time I was looking for male role-models to teach me about strength, passion, resilience, and standing up for what I believed in. I found that in Hip Hop music, first, then in all aspects of the culture (such as DJing, breakdancing, and graffiti writing), but the music, primarily the lyrics, is what I connected with the most. I was bullied a lot when I was younger, and Hip Hop was my escape that made me feel empowered. Eminem captured my feelings exactly in his song "Legacy" when he rapped about how listening to Hip Hop artists such as Onyx was a better way to cope with his issues and, at the same time, inspired him to write his own rhymes.

To this day, when I feel like I need a pep talk, when I'm not feeling my strongest and I need someone to lift me up and make me feel inspired to face my challenges head on, I turn to a Hip Hop song. As I grew up, I felt that emcees had such power in their craft and my natural talent for writing made me feel inspired to emcee. I felt such elation when I wrote rhymes, and I wanted to have that power to inspire others the way that the emcees I grew up on inspired me. I wrote my first rhymes when I was about 13 years old, and I never looked back. Today, emceeing has become such a part of me that I find myself composing rhymes in my mind or freestyling at random times throughout the day, pretty much every day.

Ahmad: What was it about Hip Hop culture, at the point you were introduced, that had the most meaningful impact on you?

Antonio: As I was describing, what had the most meaningful impact on me was the resilience and strength that I saw in the emcees. Listening to groups like Wu-Tang Clan, Mobb Deep, and Naughty By Nature, I heard stories of overcoming obstacles and rising up against all odds. Listening to Hip Hop music made me feel invincible, like I could accomplish anything. It's crazy to think that Hip Hop music changed my whole mind state, and improved my self-esteem and confidence the way it did. It is no exaggeration for me to use the popular saying, "Hip Hop saved my life." Having this experience with Hip Hop eventually Hip Hop would shape who I am today in many more ways. Feeling empowered to face my challenges and overcome the bullying that I experienced, I wanted to stand up for others and use my privilege to amplify the voices of others. In that way, Hip Hop inspired me to become an ally for the LGBTQ+ community, to become vegan and amplify the voices of the animals, to fight for gender equality and amplify the voices of women, and so much more.

Since emceeing is my element, and Hip Hop music is what I relate to and have been most influenced and impacted by, most of what I'm going to talk about in this interview will be focused on emceeing, Hip Hop music, and the voice that emcees have in the culture.

Ahmad: How would you define earth liberation? How would you define animal liberation?

Antonio: I feel that Earth liberation and animal liberation are very closely related. They are about liberating both the Earth and animals from the systems that are destructive to their existence. Earth liberation involves removing toxic pollutants and chemicals from nature, and humans changing our lifestyles to reduce our carbon footprint as much as possible. It's difficult to envision exactly what that would look like, but I know it means using clean energy sources, reconfiguring our communities to minimize the amount of energy that is needed, reimagining how we produce food, clothing, and all other items that take resources from the Earth.

Earth liberation would naturally lead to animal liberation, as reducing our carbon footprint would include adopting a vegan lifestyle. In our present world, humans cannot live in complete balance and harmony with the planet while exploiting and/or commodifying animals. Breeding animals for food purposes introduces unnecessary pollutants into the environment through the animals' waste and flatulence, as well as through the use of antibiotics in animal agriculture, and chemicals that are used to grow all of the crops needed to feed the animals. Many like to argue that we can eat animals and live in balance with the Earth and will reference ancestors in their arguments. One common example of using ancestors as an argument is when folks reference Indigenous tribes that hunted buffalo and used every part of the animal (flesh for food, bones for tools, skin for clothes), and lived in a harmonious balance with nature. The flaw with that argument is that our ancestors did not have access to the resources and information that we have today. We have new ways of producing plant-based agriculture, ways of transporting food, and ways to store food so that it lasts longer. Many of our ancestors needed to hunt for survival because they could not grow food during the winter and in times of drought. They were not able to preserve food as we can today nor were they able to easily access foods from other areas where food could be grown. With the tools and resources we have available today, there is no reason whatsoever to commodify animals. Furthermore, there is a big difference between hunting one or two animals each year to feed your family and purchasing animal flesh on a daily basis. Even in the "hunter-gatherer" days that many like to reference in their arguments against veganism, the vast majority of populations were thriving mostly on the food that they grew and gathered. Additionally, the Earth's human population is far higher than it was centuries ago when hunting was considered a sustainable practice, and the human population is growing each day. We know that the only way to sustainably feed every human is for humans to eat primarily plant-based diets. By choosing to live in a way that does not exploit or commodify animals, we can allow nature to restore homeostasis (as much as is possible at this point) on our planet, thus achieving Earth and animal liberation.

Ahmad: In your opinion, how are Hip Hop culture and Earth liberation related?

Antonio: Hip Hop culture evolved because of the ways the Earth was being exploited with new highways being built through neighborhoods. Systemic racism caused Black and Latinx folks to live in neighborhoods with less resources and less opportunities available to them. Hip Hop culture was a way Black and Latinx folks were rising from the ashes and overcoming barriers, like roses growing from concrete. Today, we still see this type of systemic racism affecting communities of color and these communities experience poorer health outcomes as a result. In response to this continued pattern of exploiting the Earth while simultaneously exploiting minorities, many people of color and Hip Hoppers alike recognize that their experiences of poverty, food deserts, lack of access to healthy food and other resources, and poor health outcomes are a result of Earth exploitation in the form of factories, concentrated animal feeding operations, pesticide use on crops (especially on crops that have been genetically modified to withstand pesticides), and oil pipelines and drilling. People within Hip Hop have become aware of this systemic racism and Earth exploitation. As a result, we recognize the need to find alternative ways of living other than using fossil fuels, animal agriculture, and other industries that harm the planet. One example of how this recognition has translated into action is the No DAPL movement in Standing Rock where various emcees including Supaman, Taboo, and Immortal Technique got involved in the protest. Another example of Hip Hop acting in Earth liberation via environmental activism occurred when a group of activists went on tour across the country in 2015 to raise awareness of environmental justice and how people of color are disproportionately affected by climate change. Emcees have also been speaking out on these issues in their lyrics for decades. A few examples are songs like Public Enemy's "Don't Give Up The Fight", dead prez's "A New Beginning", Common's "Trouble in the Water", and Reflection Eternal's "Ballad of the Black Gold" among many others.

Ahmad: In your opinion, how are Hip Hop culture and animal liberation related?

Antonio: Hip Hop and animal liberation are related in so many different ways and intersections. If we were to consolidate all that Hip Hop culture stands for and represents into four main categories, I believe they would be: expression, social justice, empowerment, and resistance. Each of these four main categories relate to animal liberation in different ways.

Expression relates to animal liberation in various ways including how people express themselves through their lifestyle, fashion, and through their art. For some, a healthy lifestyle, in and of itself, is a form of expression. Part of a healthy lifestyle includes a healthy plant-based diet which, by default, limits or eliminates animal exploitation (without getting into the weeds of the research on nutrition, there is no argument against the data that with a well-balanced diet and an adequate amount of calories, the more plants a person eats the better their health will be). Poor physical health can limit a person's expression: a b-boy/girl may dance differently if they are not in their best health; a graffiti writer may be limited in their painting; and a DJ, emcee, or beatboxer can't perform to their full potential if they are not well. Personally, I have battled with obesity, food addiction, asthma, and severe allergies for my entire life. Since changing my diet and eating more whole plant foods, I have noticed that my breath control has drastically improved, as have my stamina and energy on stage. Twelve years ago, I would have never dreamed of doing a back spin, as I could barely climb multiple flights of stairs, so expressing myself through dance was pretty much out of the question for me due to my physical health. Expression of self through art can flourish if the artist is in good health. I'm not suggesting that folks are not able to dance, sing, paint, and express themselves without being able bodied. I'm illustrating that we sometimes add additional limitations to our expression by not taking care of our physical health. Many of us remember the tragic death of the Fat Boys' Human Beatbox, who suffered a heart attack after performing one of his beatboxes; his lack of physical health not only may have ended his life much too soon, but may also have limited his expression of self through art. Many others have had their lives end too soon possibly due to lack of physical health such as Big Punisher and Heavy D. I recognize that there is a fine line between believing that we should not be comfortable with disease and being fatphobic, as well as the complexity of obesity and the social determinants of health. I'm not attempting to point the finger at anyone for not taking care of their health and I acknowledge that many others have lost their lives too soon to disorders that may have not been linked to their diet. With that said, speaking from personal experience with my physical health, and working with clients as a health educator and fitness instructor, I feel that it is worth exploring how our diet relates to our ability to express ourselves. I definitely recognize that we are all limited by our bodies' abilities as we are all differently abled; what I am saying is that when we are in our best physical health possible, we can best express ourselves through art.

Another form of expression in Hip Hop is through fashion. When fashion choices go beyond just the aesthetics, such as considering where clothing materials are sourced from, it adds to the expression. Many intentionally choose faux fur and vegan leather to make a statement about sustainability and/or compassion. RZA of the Wu-Tang Clan took this commitment to another level when he made his new 36 Chambers clothing line all vegan, including vegan leather products. Additionally, as a way to make a statement about social justice, many people choose clothing that is made from ethically sourced cotton, printed with ethically sourced inks, and assembled and sewn by individuals who were paid fair wages and offered fair working conditions. Furthermore, Hip Hop as a culture has reflected a desire to go against the grain as a countercultural force, and the ways that individuals in the Hip Hop community express themselves through clothing reflects that desire. Living a vegan lifestyle is also countercultural and going against systems that are designed to keep minority communities down. Thus, at its core, Hip Hop aligns with and relates to many of the ideals in the animal liberation movement.

Social Justice movements in Hip Hop relate to animal liberation both directly and indirectly. Some of the more prominent social justice themes that show up in Hip Hop culture include changing systems of oppression. For instance, the government's war on drugs and how it affects people of color, the struggle for financial freedom, and challenging social norms are constant themes within Hip Hop culture. Each of these social justice themes include direct action that relates to animal liberation. For example, part of challenging the concentrated animal feeding operations being strategically placed in communities of color includes boycotting the foods produced by these operations, which liberates the animals being exploited for food. Another example is how the struggle for financial freedom can be better achieved by cutting animal-based foods out of your diet in order to not only save money on your grocery bill, but also to free ourselves from the need for costly healthcare. Many people incorrectly believe that a vegan diet is more expensive to maintain; I always think these people never listened to Boogie Down Productions back in the day, who illustrated in their song "Love's Gonna Get'cha (Material Love)" that families had to subsist on cheap food options like beans, rice, and bread, and that drug selling enabled people to get paid to the point where they can add steak to the beans and rice. 2Pac spoke a lot about these social justice movements. His lyrics explored how the war on drugs, poverty, and incarceration disproportionately affected black people. In songs like "Changes" he spoke about the need to change our ways and even explicitly stated that we need to change the way we eat. Based on his legacy of being such a revolutionary and trailblazer for change, as well as his statement about changing the way we eat, I like to argue that if 2Pac were alive today he would be vegan and a strong voice for Earth and animal liberation.

Hip Hop has been about empowerment since its inception. The culture was about folks feeling empowered to overcome the barriers to success that were placed in their way as a result of systemic racism. For folks struggling to make it, empowerment is mostly about survival. Emcees such as Mobb Deep illustrated the struggle to survive with their lyrics and explored the notion of "survival of the fittest"; they believed that in their environment, only the strong survive. Some of the most impactful ways to become self-empowered, to thrive and not merely survive, include striving for personal health by eliminating animal-based foods, becoming educated about where food comes from, how food is produced, and how food production impacts our health and well-being. During the last years of Prodigy's life, he talked about how he understood that eating a healthy diet and eating more plant-based foods impacted his sickle cell anemia, and he would get sick much more often when he wasn't taking care of himself. Other examples of self-empowerment which lead to animal liberation are working together as communities to be self-sustaining rather than depending on the government for food, such as creating community gardening projects. Also, self-empowerment can encompass increasing access to healthy foods and combating food deserts that result from systemic racism.

In addition to expression, social justice, and empowerment, Hip Hop is also about resistance. Resistance in Hip Hop relates to all of the other themes discussed, but stands on its own as a premise of, as Public Enemy said, fighting the power; fighting systemic racism and challenging social norms is at the core of resistance in Hip Hop. Liberating animals through living a vegan lifestyle works to fight the power on different levels. Systemic racism runs so deep in American culture that it made its way into the USDA dietary guidelines for Americans. The guidelines state that everyone should have 3 servings of dairy per day, one with each meal. When examining rates of lactose intolerance broken down by race and ethnicity, it becomes clear that this recommendation encourages people to consume food that their bodies will reject. It is also important to acknowledge that lactose intolerance disproportionately affects people of color. Depending on what particular study you look at, from 80–90% of black folks, 60–70% of Latinx folks, and upwards of 90% of Native American folks are lactose intolerant compared to about 15% of white folks. Examining how lactose intolerance affects the vast majority of people of color while not affecting the majority of white folks, it becomes clear that the USDA dietary guidelines, which state that every American should consume at least 3 servings of dairy each day, is a form of systemic racism. By boycotting the dairy industry, we can both challenge this systemic racism while also liberating the cows from being exploited for their milk.

Ahmad: In what ways do you use aspects of Hip Hop culture to address Earth and animal liberation?

Antonio: I use Hip Hop culture to address Earth and animal liberation both in my self-expression as an emcee, and also in my work as an educator and activist. I incorporate lyrics about Earth and animal liberation in my songs on a regular basis, and I co-host and promote Hip Hop events with the goal of spreading messages about Earth and animal liberation.

When I first started recording songs back in 2005, I used to write lyrics about animal liberation mostly in the way of talking about cutting meat out of my diet. In recent years, I've really added more Earth/animal liberation themes to my lyrics and even released an entire song about veganism titled "So Many Reasons" where I talk about all the different reasons there are to live vegan including an entire verse about animal liberation and another verse about Earth liberation. I notice that when I perform this song it often serves as a conversation starter when I get off stage, as many times folks from the crowd will come up to me and ask questions about my lyrics and want to learn more. I also have more songs in the works that further explore environmental justice, and Earth/animal liberation.

As far as using Hip Hop culture in my activism, I co-founded an event series in my hometown of Albuquerque, New Mexico called *Conscious Eating & Hip Hop (CEHH)* with Victor Flores of our local Vegan Outreach Chapter. *CEHH* is a series of community events to bring folks together to share music, food, and good vibes. *CEHH* also serves as a platform for activists and educators, such as Victor and I, to share information about how non-vegan lifestyles impact the earth, the animals, our health, and disproportionately affect people of color. Each event includes a DJ and/or live beats, free vegan dinner, a Q&A session with a panel of vegan activists, and live performances. An all-vegan dinner is served to introduce participants to new vegan foods and to dispel myths about vegan food being bland and distasteful. The Q&A session consists of attendees asking vegan activists various questions; these questions may be about anything the crowd wants to know about veganism including ethics, health, environment, social justice, finances, grocery shopping, and vegan dining. Local Hip Hop acts are booked at each event and provide live performances, usually to close out the event. People always leave the event asking further questions, taking resources (fact sheets, vegan starter kits, shopping guides), and I definitely feel that the events, at the very least, plant seeds in peoples' minds about changing their lifestyles. I have had people reach out to me days after an event asking follow-up questions such as if I can send a recipe that was talked about at the event or asking me to help them choose a plant-based milk at the grocery store.

Ahmad: In your opinion, what boundaries and topics in Earth and animal liberation has Hip Hop culture yet to consider and explore?

Antonio: Personally, I don't think that Hip Hop focuses enough on animal liberation. In terms of talking about reducing animal exploitation, I feel like the focus is usually on improving personal health or saving the environment. I don't feel like there are a lot of voices in the Hip Hop community talking specifically about animal liberation. There has been some discussion about how not eating animals saves animals, and the hardships that farm animals face as a result of animal agriculture, but I feel that it hasn't been focused on or explored enough. There are also additional topics to explore including wildlife protection, the connection between the environment and wildlife, and how animal agriculture is the leading cause of species extinction. The *Hip-Hop is Green* movement founded by Keith Tucker does acknowledge animal rights as one of the six pillars of the 10th element of Hip Hop (I'll talk about that more later) and I'm hoping they will push the boundaries on what the culture addresses in regard to animal liberation; I am excited to see what the future holds for their work.

I also think that the culture hasn't fully considered the social justice aspects of veganism. There could be more discussion about topics such as how animal agriculture disproportionately affects people of color and the racist food guidelines for Americans. There could also be more awareness about the economics of our current food system and how pharmaceutical companies are profiting on multiple levels of the system, first by selling drugs to farmers for their animals and then by selling drugs to humans to treat conditions that arise as a result of eating the animals that the pharmaceutical companies already profited from. There are additional aspects of exploiting animals that I don't feel Hip Hop has even considered yet, such as how prisoner labor is used to run dairy farms. I would say the Hip Hop community is well aware of the thirteenth amendment, essentially allowing prisoners to be exploited for labor, but I have not heard much discussion about the direct link to the food system and how we may be supporting the prison industrial complex and prisoner labor through the foods we purchase.

I know that the *Hip-Hop is Green* movement is also working to address food justice and perhaps will be moving the culture in this direction in the near future, but I feel at this moment that we as a culture have some work to do in terms of learning and teaching about animal liberation.

Ahmad: Who do you see as some of the more insightful and provocative voices in Hip Hop discussing Earth and animal liberation?

Antonio: There are many emcees and other members of the Hip Hop community that have discussed Earth and animal liberation in one form or another. I feel that one of the strongest and most insightful voices in Hip Hop discussing earth and animal liberation right now is Dead Prez, specifically Stic Man. Stic has obviously been talking about veganism since the *Let's Get Free* album, but he's kept the movement going and now has the RBG Fit Club movement and podcast. His main focus is still health and well-being, but topics of Earth/animal liberation come up naturally in the conversations and he continues to drop knowledge about environmental health and ethics.

Another very prominent voice in Hip Hop talking about these issues is Keith Tucker, the founder of the *Hip-Hip is Green* movement which initiated the proclamation declaring health and wellness as the 10th element of Hip Hop. The proclamation addresses how our food choices relate to the environment and acknowledges Hip Hop's responsibility to protect the earth and live in perfect balance with nature. The 10th element contains six pillars, one of which is animal rights. *Hip-Hop is Green* organizes tours and events spreading the messages contained within the 10th element proclamation.

Additionally, as I mentioned earlier, Wu-Tang Clan members are also making moves for the vegan movement by speaking on the issues and also taking direct action, such as RZA's vegan clothing line and RZA, GZA, and Ghostface Killah teaming up with Impossible Foods and White Castle to promote plant-based sliders. Styles P is another emcee that has been using his status in Hip Hop and his assets to increase awareness and improve access to healthy foods by opening up Juice Bars in low income neighborhoods. An Atlanta emcee named

Grey, through his *Plant Based Drippin'* brand, has been making noise in Hip Hop and talking about animal liberation through some of his music including his song "Vegan Thanksgiving" that went viral in 2016. I also consider myself, an up-and-coming emcee, to be a voice in Hip Hop for Earth and animal liberation through my music, my work as a plant-based eating educator, and my activism.

CHAPTER EIGHT

Interview with
Jared A. Ball

AHMAD WASHINGTON

Ahmad: How, if at all, did Hip Hop influence you to be a scholar and an activist?

Jared: I wouldn't say Hip Hop influenced me to be a scholar or to ever at any time be an activist. Hip Hop educates me, inspires me, informs me and continues to provide ways and means to understand and explain the world. But I was born into a political and intellectual household, raised by a political and intellectual mother and inspired by positive mythologies around her family's labor organizing, communism and atheism and my father's activism in the Black liberation and labor struggles. Hip Hop supplemented those interests and helped me find historic and contemporary examples of people and organizations doing related work. Hip Hop also gives me ideas for developing, challenging and building upon those ideas and politics while also exposing the contradictions and obstacles.

Now, I do think it is important to point out that while not encouraging me directly to activism, Hip Hop has indirectly helped me shape my outlook, self-concept and has been instrumental in simply showing me that being strong, loud, different and aggressive is both necessary and acceptable. This is essential to activist and academic work, especially the kinds that I am interested in.

Ahmad: What was the first element of Hip Hop you became interested in and why?

Jared: Easy. The DJ. I am a former wannabe drummer. My first love since child-hood are the drums. And I was born in 1971, in Washington, D.C., where Go-Go—simply the best pocket rhythm in the world with Salsa not far behind—was/is big and where percussion and live bands rule(d). There was no Hip Hop then. I can still remember a time where there was no Hip Hop, certainly none as wildly promoted and distributed as is the case now, so when Hip Hop emerged I was already set to a default that would have me look for the equivalent of the drummer in that formation. I deeply appreciate all the elements; I loved the graffiti I saw in films and on trains and walls during visits to New York City as a child; I loved and tried (failing miserably) to mimic the b-girls/boys, and I still freestyle when alone and think I'm nice on a mic that no one else hears. But it's always been those turntables, the half-on and off headphones and tilted head of the DJ, the cuts, the breaks, the juggles, the centerpiece of the party, even when not necessarily seen or recognized. That gets my attention. To this day, whenever I go see a band live, I have to position myself to watch the drummer(s) and whenever a DJ is present (not always the case anymore) that's who I want to be able to see at a show. I have always loved tracks that featured scratching and videos that showed the DJ doing their thing. And its why, to this day, Premier and Pete Rock are my top two of all time DJ/producers who almost always feature some tight cuts (and incredible high-level sampling).

Ahmad: In your opinion how has Hip Hop influenced politics and politicians for the good or bad?

Jared: This is where I find myself most often in disagreement with my peers. I think some want to give an undo power or difference to Hip Hop. Like it is somehow magical in a way other forms of expression are not. That is simply not true. Hip Hop is no different than any other form of cultural expression in that it is: A) produced in a broader sociopolitical context, in this case by colonized, oppressed communities who are themselves not free or in control over anything they produce—including art, its production, popularization and not at all the wealth extracted, and therefore, B) Hip Hop, like any other cultural expression, produces a variety of politics and influences a variety of people to do a variety of things. Hip Hop has been used to support the most radical of politics and to sup-port their development and dissemination. However, Hip Hop is also largely now the unwitting or unknown carriers of the worst of capitalist, white supremacist and anti-woman politics and agendas.

For instance, Hip Hop has been used politically by the Democratic Party (a ton!) via campaigns led by mainstream commercial artists like Sean Combs and "Vote Or Die," and an endless parade of commercial artists were brought out or came out for Barack Obama in 2008 and 2012 and then, to a lesser extent, for Hilary Clinton and Bernie Sanders in 2016. Lesser known were the artists like

Tef Poe or Skipp Coon before him who were wildly critical of the Democratic Party and those candidates. And even lesser known than that were/are the artists who supported ventures to the Left of those, say, Marcel P. Black, or The Cornel West Theory or Dead Prez and others who supported everything from new party formation to Green Party campaigns to nothing at all as it pertains to voting.

As I write this Pharrell Williams is currently working with a PR firm to promote that people vote for the Democratic Party. This, of course, has been a strategy for years and is not new but does demonstrate the consistent deployment of famous artists by the very political forces that help create and maintain the inequality from which these rappers come. A few years ago, I was in a number of arguments around artists supporting Obama or Hillary Clinton forgetting that she spoke openly while Secretary of State of using Hip Hop, as jazz had been in the 1950s, to promote a positive image of the United States locally to oppressed communities and internationally in the hopes of easing its foreign policy.

People I've considered friends, comrades or simply who have inspired me for years have been put to these efforts. They may be incredible artists, truly, but what Hip Hop nation or body said it was ok for them to be State Department spokespeople for Hip Hop? What collective platform are they carrying and with what politics? And then, of course, who benefits? Clearly, it's not Black people given that the material conditions they face continue to be wretched. And look now at Kanye West. He claims to speak for Hip Hop and the world as he supports the man Busta Rhymes appropriately called Agent Orange. Hip Hop has never organized and developed a clear politics and this is why all manner of everything is promoted by those using its various elements.

I've argued, and will continue to, that it's more important to focus on the politics and commercial structure that produces the fame and platform of the artists rather than the often politically useless things they say or do. In fact, again, I continue to argue that the only reason popular culture and fame exists at all is to perform the political duties of managing public opinion and often distorting public political discussion. To vaguely over-simplify my argument, we do need to understand that regardless of their talent or whether we like their work, artists like Snoop only have their fame or careers so that ultimately he could be used to speak out as he did recently against Colin Kaepernick. Kanye West's career was developed by an industry specifically so he could be used now to defend Agent Orange, or that is, to speak out against the intentionally-made-lesser-famous-tendencies in Hip Hop to do as Busta Rhymes and A Tribe Called Quest did and shame a country that would elect such a monster. Beyonce's primary political function is to redefine Black womanhood and radical politics away from those like Assata Shakur or Ramona Africa. These are brilliantly talented people but their fame is conferred upon them for their political function, not their talent. No one has ever survived being simultaneously rich, famous and radically political. There are no exceptions to this rule yet. None.

In fact, and further, there is no such thing as "entertainment." Everything is politics and everything is commercial product. From art to artists, to the ideas and politics they promote. Better yet, to paraphrase those who study the science of propaganda, entertainment is best understood as the primary method by which those in power communicate with the rest of us. No one is famous without the support of really just about three companies which themselves are connected to—and relatively small parts of—international conglomerates. Lucian Grainge is widely known in business circles as "the most powerful man in music." But who knows his name? We only know the names of the artists he has assured become famous and whose fame is connected to more than talent but to an ability to promote a particular set of ideas almost all of which encourage shopping, violence directed at Black, Native and Brown people only and messages demeaning women.

All of my work regarding Hip Hop and pop culture has been focused on the ways in which Kwame Ture remains right that, "Black visibility is not Black Power." In other words, all this popularity of Black people and art has meant nothing in terms of redistributing wealth and power to those same Black communities. So, Hip Hop may indeed promote Black images but it is controlled by a corporate structure which allows for elite white men to determine which forms of the culture we get and how much and who gets to be heard and largely what they will say.

So, sure, there have been and are indeed some revolutionary politics expressed and some progressive influence over many of us in many areas of life. But clearly, just by looking at the realities we all still face, there has been no revolution and no explosion of a permanent and well-organized radical movement overthrowing inequality and institutionalizing radical changes. That is, of course, not Hip Hop's fault but it is also to say that the idea, which I think is promoted through a false narrative of Hip Hop's history—a narrative which says that Hip Hop has somehow led to some new world with new opportunity and equality—is absolutely bogus, phony, fugazi, and unreal.

Ahmad: Hip Hop activism is a term that is somewhat new and emerging rapidly since 2011. What do you consider Hip Hop activism and not and what makes Hip Hop activism different than other forms of activism?

Jared: I hope this is cool but I have to try to address questions four through seven, together. I have always hated the phrase "Hip Hop activist" and have had a longstanding struggle with how that phrase has been defined and how it has been used or abused. I think the phrase was intentionally advocated by those not wanting to maintain any connection to existing and incomplete liberation struggles, particularly those of the Black Power era variety, including those of the radical Latinx and Chicanx movements. From the Harry Allen phrase, "Raptivist," I think the phrase "Hip Hop activist" has been developed to further the disconnection of Hip Hop from the Black and Brown and colonized communities from which it all emerged. So, instead of people being able to focus on those communities, and specifically their most radical political traditions, we were/are all encouraged into thinking of some ill-defined, amorphous, ambiguous thing called, Hip Hop.

I also think that the timing described in the questions is a bit off in that the phrase, Hip Hip Hop activist, is older and has lost popularity and use over time as its been replaced by newer forms of the same problem, be it Black Lives Matter, MeToo, or now the school shootings and environment movements. I don't think many today organize under the banner of Hip Hop as was done in the 1990s and early 2000s, but the problems, as I see them, are the same in that there is little clarity over ideology and politics, a preference to avoid race and class (far more than gender or sexuality at this point) and a near erasure of the most radical elements of Black and other liberation struggles. In other words, there has always been the problem of it being more preferable and easy to do work under the guise of a commercialized pop version of Dr. King than it has ever been to do so under the banner of say George Jackson (or shoot, even the real Dr. King who I will say again is the most known and least understood figure in human history second maybe and only maybe to the historical Jesus Christ). Even today, the "Assata Taught Me," worn on tees and hoodies by many has not translated in any meaningful way to a deep engagement with the politics of scientific socialism, internationalism, armed struggle, etc. and I've had arguments with friends and former friends now over even publishing an open letter on his request from political prisoner and Shakur comrade Jalil Muntaqim in which he asked, very critically, what people thought they were doing under her name.

But it is like the late Amiri Baraka once said to Bill Fletcher in their debate over the book on Malcolm X attributed to Dr. Manning Marable. Baraka told Fletcher to stop hiding his real arguments over ideology and politics behind obviously flawed claims of jealousy or fears of real histories. "Put your ideology on the table," Baraka told him. And that is what needs still to be done among those claiming some form of Hip Hop activism. I think the phrase has become a euphemism for non-profit, Democratic Party operative politics. And if that is what folks want, fine, claim it, so that I and others can openly argue against that formation and we can become clear through debate and compromise and strategy and tactics about how we are going to get where we claim we want to go.

I have and do appreciate that there are a great many who have adopted various approaches to the phrase and who have sought to have Hip Hop be that catalyst for their own activism but the phrase I think has been promoted to take race out of the center of people's organizing and to walk people away from traditions of radical political struggle which has been the desire of those in power for a good long time. It has also allowed for any number of co-optive abuses and continues to this day to confuse or disassociate people from radical political ideas or from clarifying—even acknowledging—their own ideology. This is why we see some silly groups with Hip Hop in their name which is really just a signal to White liberal money that they are safe to fund. It is like when Black radio became "Urban" radio so they could get White ad money. Funny how those "urbans" still live real separate and "urban."

A few years ago, while still hosting radio, I tried to engage some notables on this subject directly. I argued in separate occasions, but similarly with both Bakari Kitwana and Jeff Chang that Hip Hop activists, (myself included) had never clarified their politics or properly organized around them which allowed (and still allows) for groups mostly funded by a White liberal non-profit industry ("complex" as some have called it) to pick whomever that will promote softer politics, mostly around electing Democrats or some other vague voting endeavor, maybe something around the environment. These groups will be given money and media access and platforms to proclaim they speak for a Hip Hop community or nation when they are little more than an email list or Twitter handle and certainly not involved in anything meaningful, substantive or connected to traditions of radical struggle. In the end, they bring potential voters to the Democratic Party which as many have pointed out for decades is, "where radical politics go to die."

My argument remains that there is still a problem over political education and organization largely due to several factors related to the generation prior to mine being wiped out by the most powerful state in human history. The Counter Intelligence Program (COINTELPRO) destroyed the most radical and scientific organizations and left us with a bunch of mystical, religious types, hustlers and non-profit warriors none of whom are versed in or want to engage in the ideas dealt with even by those they claim in name. I mean, how many people mention Dr. King or Malcolm X and never discuss how each of them openly expressed a disdain for capitalism? People say Assata Shakur but never discuss socialism (scientific or any other form) and I KNOW people often mention Dr. Huey P. Newton but for anything other than his brilliant development of intercommunalism. I could go on and on but my point is that under an undefined label of Hip Hop activist most can avoid claiming, studying or advancing radical ideas and can avoid any overt discussion of race or colonialism.

I am still bothered by my memory of standing in the convention hall for the 2004 National Hip-Hop Convention watching a Hip Hop activist movement of the Hip Hop nation, saying we need to get in line and vote for John Kerry. All these years of work and argument and this was the grand outcome? And since then, where are we? Hip Hop has produced no candidate; I was, in fact, once called the first Hip Hop presidential candidate for my initial run for the Green

Party nomination in 2007 before I stepped back to support Cynthia McKinney and Rosa Clemente. Most notables then, from Davey D to Kitwana, to Chang to whomever else, all said we needed to support Barack Obama, an idea which I think has since been proven wrong, but while I am happily immature enough to say "I told you so", I am also aware now, as I was then, that the problem was that I was not a candidate put forth by a clear convention style vote of the Hip Hop nation. I was an individual running under a banner of Hip Hop activist with my own brand of what that meant/means. It was doomed to failure for that reason alone. And this is a problem still unsolved.

There is no national organized body of the Hip Hop community (whatever that means) which determines who and it what ways anyone will speak for the whole. There are no political candidates running on clear platforms put together by Hip Hop for Hip Hop. Hip Hop doesn't even own or control its product and cannot organize support for its own community. This is why I once, and still argue, that if there is a Hip Hop Nation it must be understood that it, like that Black and Brown communities from which it comes, is colonized and must, on that basis, begin to organize and address itself to the world. This imposed narrative that we get from pop history books and film is that Hip Hop emerged from the slums and over time took over making the world ready for a Black president and for Black famous people to be welcomed. But, this is absurd. I mean Dan Charnas wrote a very popular book on Hip Hop history and called Hip Hop "an American success story." Unless he meant success for American corporations in exploiting and maintaining and even presiding over a worsening exploitation of a community is a success, then he simply furthers this absurd myth that, as Bob Brown has said of bad ideas, should be "shotgunned."

Hip Hop emerged from colonized communities who, from the first Sylvia Robinson record deal, have been trapped in a full corporate, commercial and fraudulent industry which creates phony versions of ourselves often used then to justify public policy which keeps us in unequal and oppressed conditions. Even Robinson's formation of the Sugar Hill Gang, a record people still praise for "opening up doors," was comprised of phony rappers stealing names and rhymes from less marketable MCs. The door Robinson helped open was the one that gave entry to a goldmine to be stripped and stolen. After 50 years of Hip Hop making billions for White international conglomerates, most owned by conservatives who use their wealth to produce state policies which increase the inequalities faced by most of us, Black people are no better off and if we break out the real economic data, we will see things are actually worse now. Oppressed people do not simply produce an art form that oppressors love and then, therefore, use to confer power back over to the oppressed. No, the cultural expression of the oppressed is cultivated into a form that is used against them as is the case today.

No, Hip Hop activism is no different than any other form. It needs to clarify its politics because it is currently used by anyone, from rabid capitalists to those of us righteously interested in revolutionary politics.

Ahmad: Do you think all Hip Hop elements and individuals are political in nature?

Jared: While I do think everything is political, I do not think anything or anyone is inherently political. People and art forms are politicized one way or another which is why I said previously that we need to be clear about where we want to go. If I am not clear, my children will be politicized by someone or something else. We are not in control of institutions; we have no political power and we have no wealth. Our only hope is in our ability to be radicalized and to organize collectively around those politics.

Ahmad: What was the most politically repressive act toward Hip Hop activists has been?

Jared: Generally, I don't think there has been any act most repressive to *Hip Hop activists in particular.* What is happening is happening to us all and the absence of clarity has been a problem for us all. I think, though, that what has happened to Hip Hop has happened and is happening to everyone with particularly harmful effects for the most colonized and oppressed, or those from whom Hip Hop comes. That is, we are all suffering from an increasingly sophisticated delivery of White supremacy, capitalism and male dominance, fostered by a propaganda system the likes the world has never seen. I might define, then, the most repressive act toward Hip Hop being the corruption of its popular form into one that defends and supports the very processes which create the poverty, police violence, political and general mass incarceration, repression of radical ideas and so on. This corruption of the popular form of Hip Hop is not just in total control over a preponderance of its lyrical and visual content but in a narrative that has been developed alongside the art that suggests Hip Hop has helped us overcome something or has helped us circumvent capitalism by offering avenues to wealth or job creation. This, given the economic details and condition we face, is objectively and patently untrue and ridiculous as even a suggestion.

But! If there was one thing I would want to point to in terms of how the broader political machinery has impacted Hip Hop, I'd probably point to the encroachment over the years of copyright law. Most are not aware that copyright, a subset of intellectual property rights, is easily among this country's biggest industries. In other words, the ownership and control over ideas is paramount. Copyright law has allowed for non-artist owners of the work to control and procure payment from all kinds of sources for use of someone else's intellectual or artistic production. Almost no artists own their own music. Those who do can determine if it is heard or who gets paid when it is played. But it's worse than even the theft of the money. Copyright has literally changed the sound of Hip Hop largely through lawsuits over sampling. This is why so much today is not sample based but keyboard and digital concoctions. Like it or not, this is not some natural shift in the art; it is a direct result of people not being able to afford the enormous fees to sample one drum or bass line. Now I have to forever miss my boom bap—or get it from those beneath the pop cultural world like Oddisee.

Yea, that would be it. That goddamned copyright law stuff. I hate it.

Afterword

DAVID MICHAEL

"Y'all closed already?", a neighborhood boy, who I've never seen before, asks me as I lock the gates to the Green Haven Community Garden.

"Yeah, we'll be back."

"You the boss right?"

"Yeah, something like that."

My name is David Michael. I've been an activist in South Florida for five years. Prior to that, I was incarcerated for eight years. During my time in prison, I began to educate myself on the judicial system, the brainwashing of Black folks and the hidden knowledge that many people choose to ignore in their daily life. I began to wake up to the questionable conditions that have been happening in our society for many years. I felt compelled to do something about this. I began to embark on the journey of changing my perspective and how I interact with my community. In order to do better, you must know better. How can you change anything if we do not actively know what is going on? This is where knowledge of history and wisdom of "self-combine" to make positive changes. A lot of people talk about what is wrong in the world, but not a lot of people are willing to get their hands dirty.

While watching an interview on [the MC] Prodigy (of Mobb Deep), he began discussing the history of slave food, the relationship of current food trends within poor Black communities and what is needed to be done in order to bring awareness to the common folk. I began researching the food system and controversial topics such as GMO and meat consumption. My interest in food trends led to an interest in gardening. Word of my new fascination spread though the grapevine and soon I began working at a youth recreation center in Overtown, a low-income neighborhood, doing gardening classes. I learned alongside the kids. When I spoke to them about gardening and growing their own food, I began to see personal power.

Gardening is a term most people use when talking about plant-related activities. What we do is considered Urban Farming. Urban Farming means being in the hood, and educating the people. It is being in the concrete jungles of urban areas, and making a green space. It is making people of the ghetto aware of the power they possess when they take control of their health. The lack of access to affordable, wholesome foods with no nutritional value is knows as a Food Desert. Why don't you find a Whole Foods in the hood? Or a vegan spot? The system has been designed to make these people to depend on corner stores and fast food. In response, the Black community has the highest level of diabetes, high blood pressure, and other diseases. These illnesses are in-fact due to nutritional deficiencies. But the majority of people do not know this. So they take medicine, which contributes to further illnesses, when all they really need to do is change their diet. However, this is not easy [financially] in all areas of the city.

In 2018, the Overtown Green Haven Community Project was created to bring awareness to a huge economic issue in one of Miami's oldest neighborhoods. Once a thriving historic center for commerce in the Black community, Overtown is now considered one of these food dessert. The Green Haven Community Project aims to empower local residents in the pursuit of obtaining healthy, fresh, local and affordable food. To end this crisis, GHP provide residents with a space to learn and to grow their own food. It gives them a sense of community. Urban fruit and vegetable gardening has been proven to help fight back against racism, poverty, social injustice, and gentrification. Our goal is to create a more resilient Overtown community that can withstand the pressures placed on it presently and in the future. Each month, the food harvested from the garden is used to feed the homeless community in Overtown and bring all members of the community together for a day of giving.

A majority of the people that contribute to the garden and feeding events have a strong urban culture within them. Many of them whom actually are in the local Hip Hop industry. Hip Hop activism is something people can relate and connect to. Hip Hop allows creative people to express themselves in a way that is culturally appropriate for them, while addressing social issues. There is space to show a spectrum of emotions in Hip Hop music such as betrayal, neglect, passion and power. Hip Hop is probably the largest genre of music listened to in the world, for this reason, Hip Hop is also the media where the youth engage in. Combining activism with Hip Hop creates music with content and positive messages, as opposed to a lot of other Hip Hop. Activism in Hip Hop gives the youth a positive role model to look up to. When the majority of rap music speaks on murder and violence, it makes people numb when it happens in real life. There must be a group of folks to counter the bullshit.

This book will give people who are doing community work a platform. To actively speak on what is going on in their region and give other people a perspective on why it is important to be doing the work in the first goddam place. There is not a lot of people doing activist work, so the small percentage of people who are—their voices need to be heard. They are the ones taking the problems head-on and dealing with issues in the community that matter. It is imperative that we stick together as a unit, regardless of personal discrepancies If you believe in the work and the cause then you continue going. This is a marathon. Not a sprint.

The written word cannot be censored like online activism. I want people to do their own research. Don't just go off anyone's word. Look at the whole picture, don't pick and choose what your reading—read everything! Learn what your community needs. Learn what barriers you need to break in your community. Learn what YOUR people need in the community. More people need to stand up and take action. You don not have to join an organization. You can make your own organization and work with people you feel comfortable. Do something about the issues. Figure out your own gifts and contribute. Mix passion with purpose. Live in your purpose. Walk in your purpose.

Contributors

Jared A. Ball, Ph.D., is a father and husband. After that he is a Full Professor of Communication Studies at Morgan State University, a journalist, host, producer and curator of the multimedia website of emancipatory journalism imixwhatilike. org. Dr. Ball is author of *I Mix What I Like: A Mixtape Manifesto* and has published widely in academic and popular media outlets and in a variety of forms including; mixtapes, video mixtapes, podcasts, commentary and essays and in 2007 was dubbed by Free Speech Radio News as, "the first hip-hop political candidate" for his then run for the presidential nomination of the Green Party.

Katrina Benally, a Diné Native American, lesbian, Hip Hop artist, was born and raised in Gallup, New Mexico. She is one of the hardest working women in the Southwest Hip Hop scene. She has been on lineups with acts like Cappadonna, Gavlyn, Def-I, Wake Self, Young Native, and Mykki Blanco. She also spent time on Warped Tour 2016 raising funds for wells in Africa. As a part of the lesbian duo, K. Benally/LETSJUSB, she headlined at Albuquerque, New Mexico's LGBTQ Pride 2016. Her activism in her lyrics speak on matters such as police brutality, racism, and sexism. As a community organizer, she sponsors adult and youth studio time and art workshops from her own pocket.

"Mic" Crenshaw was born and raised in Chicago and Minneapolis and currently resides in Portland Oregon. Crenshaw is an independent Hip Hop artist, respected emcee, poet, educator and activist. Crenshaw is the Lead U.S. Organizer for the Afrikan HipHop Caravan and uses cultural activism as a means to develop international solidarity related to Human Rights and Justice through Hip Hop and Popular Education. In addition to his highly-acclaimed work in spoken work and Hip Hop, Mic co-founded GlobalFam, a non-profit (EducationWithOut Borders 501c3) project to create and maintain a computer center for disadvantaged youth in Burundi, Central Africa. Mic has released numerous albums available on most popular digital platforms and has toured internationally in Tanzania, Kenya, South Africa, Zimbabwe, Russia, Germany and Cuba. Crenshaw was voted Portland's Best Hip Hop Artist in 2016 by Willamette Week. In 2019 Mic Crenshaw received the Fields Artist Fellowship Award from the Oregon Community Foundation.

Arash Daneshzadeh, Ed.D., is a biracial refugee, poet, children's author, organizer, and educator from war-torn Iran. He is a faculty member at the University of San Francisco—Graduate School of Education, as well as faculty for the Prison University Project at San Quentin State Penitentiary. Dr. Daneshzadeh also serves as National Chair for Save The Kids from Incarceration, a national nonprofit focused on prison abolition and school-sanctioned violence and co-edited a textbook on the topic of youth punishment entitled Understanding, Dismantling, and Disrupting the Prison-To-School Pipeline. Dr. Daneshzadeh's recently published research based on his doctoral work at UC Davis involved an ethnographic study of Black girls participating in Restorative Justice programs at a local alternative school in the Bay Area, which focused on navigational and resistance capital among Black girls. Currently, Arash serves as Editor-In-Chief of The Transformative Justice Journal and is co-founder of the educational equity agency called Third Space Educational Consulting. Follow him on Twitter @ a_daneshzadeh or learn more about his work at DrArashDaneshzadeh.com.

Selinda Guerrero, Afro-Latina Feminist, is the Albuquerque Coordinator for Save the Kids, a national all-volunteer organization building a movement to end the school-to-prison pipeline. She leads Millions for Prisoners, the New Mexico chapter, a national movement to abolish prisons and oppressive systems in the U.S. and beyond. Organizer for Justice for Jaquise Lewis ("Albuquerque's Trayvon Martin") continuing our fight for justice. She is a Black Lives Matter organizer with Building Power for Black New Mexico. She is a single mother of six with deep roots in New Mexico. She grew up in a gang environment consisting of violence and drug activity. As a teen mother and eighth grade pushout she became active and motivated to work for change by building networks of community alliances over the last twenty-five years.

Eli Jacobs-Fantauzzi is an award-winning filmmaker who created films like "Inventos: Hip Hop Cubano" and "HomeGrown: HipLife in Ghana" he has documented Hip Hop from India to Colombia and throughout the Caribbean. A graduate of UC Berkeley, he received his MA degree from NYU Tisch School of the Arts. Currently, he is working on a transmedia project called "Defend Puerto Rico" and is curating the 9th Annual Fist Up Film Festival in the Bay Area, California. His dedication to his craft is deeply connected to his commitment to social justice and the belief in the transformative power of storytelling.

Lauren Leigh Kelly, Ph.D., is an Assistant Professor of Urban Teacher Education at Rutgers University Graduate School of Education. Her research is focused on critical Hip Hop literacies, critical consciousness development, Black feminist theory, and culturally responsive pedagogy. Kelly received her doctorate in English Education from Teachers College, Columbia University and taught high school English for ten years in New York where she also developed courses in spoken-word poetry, Hip Hop literature and culture, and theatre arts. Her work has been published in academic journals and featured in Education Week, Education Update, and School Library Journal.

David Michael is a community activist that feeds the homeless and also gives back to the community by putting on events for the Youth he has ran two successful programs such as teaching the youth how to grow there own food and mentoring kids in the foster care system

Anthony J. Nocella II, Ph.D., is an Assistant Professor in the Department of Criminal Justice and Criminology at Salt Lake Community College and founder of the Lowrider Studies Journal. He is the editor and founder of the Peace Studies Journal, Transformative Justice Journal, and co-editor of five book series including Critical Animal Studies and Theory with Lexington Books and Hip Hop Studies and Activism with Peter Lang Publishing. He has published over fifty book chapters or articles and forty books. Nocella is the National Coordinator of Save the Kids, Executive Director of the Institute for Critical Animal Studies, Director of the Academy for Peace Education, and acquisitions editor of Arissa Media Group. His website is www.anthonynocella.org.

Tony Quintana, also known by his stage name I.Q. the Professor, is an activist, educator, and emcee from Albuquerque, NM. He has worked in the field of Health Education for over 10 years and has managed health promotion programs focusing on a wide variety of topics including nutrition, fitness, diabetes, obesity, and HIV. He is also an experienced fitness instructor and has led fitness programs in a variety of settings. Tony has been vegetarian since 2007, vegan since 2016, and enjoys sharing information on the many benefits of a plant-based diet through education, activism, and music.

Reies Romero lives in the Twin Cities and is a Hip Hop Activist, DJ, Teacher, Social Worker and Promoter of the Annual Twin Cities DillaDay Celebration as well as head of Entertainment for the Twin Cities Day of Dignity. He is the Director of the James Dewitt Yancey Foundation MN Chapter and Co-founder of the Universal Movement for the Advancement of Hip Hop, also the Leader of the Omega Zulu's Twin Cities (Zulu Union). Reies is the Marketing Coordinator for the Muslim Youth Leadership Awards and a Certified Speaker with Islamic Resource Group. Reies is the former National Director for Save the Kids and believes in the principles of ending all youth incarnation and abolishment of police. Reies facilitates workshops and presentations on Hip Hop History, Direct Activism, History of Djing, History of Islam in America and the West and much.

Nathaniel "N8" Sanders is a twenty-two year-old college student, currently attending Salt Lake Community College pursuing the Film Production Technician (AAS) degree. Before starting his SLCC 2018 fall enrollment, Nate attended the University of Utah from fall 2015 to spring 2018, being involved in a film club and taking multiple film-related courses. He had an actor role in a 2016 short webisode series titled Eight Zero One. He currently has four years of experience editing (mainly with Adobe Premiere Pro and After Effects), and three years of acting experience. He likes a mix of both. He's had a passion for film since the age of twelve, and aims to impact the world with powerful messages through film. He has edited and contributed to several short films and a thirty minute documentary, and worked a short internship with Sundance in 2019.

Clifton G. Sanders, Ph.D., received his doctorate from University of Utah and his bachelors from Hamline University. Sanders is the Provost for Academic Affairs at Salt Lake Community College. He has more than 25 years teaching, administrative and leadership experience in higher education. He led the development of several STEM programs and is a collaborator on several local, regional and national initiatives on education, diversity and inclusivity, and workforce development. His scientific work resulted in six patents in biomaterials technology. He is a University of Utah Chemistry Department Distinguished Alumnus, and he coauthored a 2009 paper on music and democracy published in *Radical Philosophy Review*.

Don C. Sawyer III, Ph.D. serves as Vice President for Equity and Inclusion and is an associate professor of sociology at Quinnipiac University. He teaches the university's first sociology course dedicated to Hip Hop culture. He earned his Ph.D. in Sociology and M.S. in Education from Syracuse University and a B.A. in Psychology from Hartwick College. His scholarly interests include race, urban education, Hip Hop culture/pedagogy, critical media literacy, and visual sociology.

Chandra Ward, Ph.D., is an Assistant Professor of Sociology at the University of Tennessee at Chattanooga teaching urban sociology and a number of other sociological topics. Her research is guided by the philosophy of helping to amplify traditionally marginalized voices. This is evident in her research on public housing residents and her textbook, an intersectional introduction to sociology reader titled, Voices From the Margin: Fresh perspectives on an introduction to sociology." Professor Ward also uses photography and social media to help make sociology accessible to those outside of academia. It can be found here at sociologysocialshutter.blogspot.com.

Ahmad Washington Ph.D., N.C.C., is an Assistant Professor in the Department of Counseling and Human Development at The University of Louisville. His research interests include African American males' ethnic and gender identity development and social justice school counseling interventions. Dr. Washington has either contributed to or produced independently more than 30 manuscripts and national, regional and state presentations. He is co-editor of the recent book, Black male student success in 21st century urban schools: School counseling for equity, access and achievement. Additionally, Dr. Washington has received various counseling related awards including the First Annual Association of Multicultural Counseling and Development Asa Hilliard Scholarship Award (2009).

Index

www.ingramcontent.com/pod-product-compliance
Lightning Source LLC
Chambersburg PA
CBHW050617280326
41932CB00016B/3079